THE

PERFORMER'S VOICE

THE

PERFORMER'S

VOICE

Realizing Your Vocal Potential

Meribeth Bunch Dayme

W. W. NORTON & COMPANY

New York   London

W. W. Norton & Company has been independent since its founding in 1923, when William Warder Norton and Mary D. Herter Norton first published lectures delivered at the People's Institute, the adult education division of New York City's Cooper Union. The Nortons soon expanded their program beyond the Institute, publishing books by celebrated academics from America and abroad. By mid-century, the two major pillars of Norton's publishing program—trade books and college texts—were firmly established. In the 1950s, the Norton family transferred control of the company to its employees, and today—with a staff of four hundred and a comparable number of trade, college, and professional titles published each year—W. W. Norton & Company stands as the largest and oldest publishing house owned wholly by its employees.

Figures I.1, 2.1, 4.1, 4.3, 4.5, 5.1, 5.2, 5.3, 5.4, 6.1, 6.2, 6.4, and 6.5 are reprinted with kind permission of Springer-Verlag and M. Bunch. From *Dynamics of the Singing Voice,* M. Bunch. Figures 1.1, 1.3, 2.2, 3.2, and 3.3 are modeled after *Anatomy of Movement,* Blandine Calais-Germain.

The text of this book is composed in Fairfield
with the display set in Belucian.
Composition and new illustrations by ElectraGraphics, Inc.
Book design by Jo Anne Metsch.
Manufacturing by the Maple-Vail Book Group.
Production manager: Benjamin Reynolds.

Library of Congress Cataloging-in-Publication Data

Bunch, Meribeth, 1938–
     The performer's voice : realizing your vocal potential / Meribeth Bunch Dayme.
          p. cm.
     Includes bibliographical references and index.
     ISBN 0-393-06136-1 (hardcover)
     1. Singing—Instruction and study. 2. Vocal music—Interpretation (Phrasing,
dynamics, etc.) I. Title.
     MT820.B859 2005
     789—dc22

                                                                    2005013697

W. W. Norton & Company, Inc., 500 Fifth Avenue, New York, N.Y. 10110
www.wwnorton.com

W. W. Norton & Company Ltd., Castle House, 75/76 Wells Street, London W1T 3QT

1 2 3 4 5 6 7 8 9 0

DEDICATED TO THE CREATIVE,

ARTISTIC, AND HEALING CAPACITIES

IN EVERY PERFORMER

Contents

Illustrations

Preface

The Performer's Voice recognizes that the very nature of the vocal arts demands a balanced approach to performance. This book is written to encourage performers, teachers, and professionals that serve the vocal arts to take a new look at the elements of exemplary performance: a presence of mind and spirit, coordination and physical efficiency, technical proficiency, expression, and imagination. The explanation and balanced approach to performance in *The Performer's Voice* will enable those in the vocal arts to use their own voices effectively and efficiently to create compelling performances and to transmit that knowledge to others.

This book is directed at a broad group of people who use their voices every day, sometimes more than they realize. This includes singers and actors, of course, but also teachers, choral directors, public speakers of all types—trial lawyers, ministers, radio announcers—and professionals who work with the voice, like speech and language therapists and ear, nose, and throat specialists. If you use your voice for your professional work, whether you are a student or already working in your chosen field, then this book is for you.

If you are a singer or an actor, this book will encourage you to become attentive to your own voice and how it functions, rather than to rely on a technique learned parrot fashion. Faulty technique or lack of understanding can come back to haunt you if you do not understand what you are doing. In general, professional performers must cope for themselves on the road, and most do not have the luxury of an accompanying teacher. The more you understand about your voice, the less you will panic in a vocal crisis.

If you are a teacher and future teacher, you have to talk more than anyone. It is your job every day. If a course in voice is not included in your training, then you need this information. Those of you who teach young people often find yourselves teaching subjects you have not studied—like singing. Knowing a few useful exercises and ways of approaching the voice will be very helpful to you.

If you are a speech therapist, you work constantly with people who have vocal problems. The more experience you have with your own voice, the better you will be able to help your client. Many therapists do not take time to experiment with their own voices—and this shows in their inability to diagnose and correct problems. Rather than being able to "see" and hear the problem, they rely on some preconceived textbook knowledge. Knowing how to use your own voice can be invaluable when you are helping someone else who may have no idea how the voice functions or how to address specific vocal problems.

If you are a doctor, then you are so busy working with people that you have hardly enough time to think. When you want to walk in your patients' shoes, however, you must do some practical voice work. This book will help you work with your own voice so that you can help your patients' better.

If you are someone who speaks for a living—a professional speaker, minister, radio or TV personality, trial lawyer—losing vocal quality could result in loss of your livelihood. Often we do not think about our voices until something goes wrong. Recovery can then mean a long road back, with layoffs from work and loss of income. This does not need to happen, provided you understand how the voice works and how to use it efficiently.

Vocal pedagogy and vocal anatomy are important parts of the curricula in performing arts programs internationally, yet there are few texts that offer an understanding of the anatomy and function of the voice coupled with practical suggestions for optimal vocal health and compelling performance. Many of these textbooks are full of important academic detail but tend to lack everyday application. To add to the challenge, explanations of the voice are often colored by preconceived ideas regarding its use and function, and it is difficult to find a straightforward, nonbiased discussion.

This book encourages a new look at the issues by giving performers and students in the vocal arts, and those voice professionals who work with them, practical guidelines for a more sustainable basis for using the voice well—healthily and imaginatively.

The Performer's Voice has three main sections, which are designed to lead the reader from the logic of the body and vocal technique to the magic of performance, beginning with the vocal instrument and finishing with the mental, spiritual, and intuitive aspects of performing and vocal health.

Part 1, "Making Sense of Vocal Mechanics," discusses the logic of the body and encourages readers to think for themselves about the function of the voice, explains as simply as possible how the voice works, and suggests ways to observe technique and improve it where necessary. Part 2, "The Art of Vocal Expression and Presentation," includes ways of improving vocal color and expressivity, as well as approaches to speaking in public, whether it is to introduce a concert or a play, present a project, argue a case, or give a public lecture. It includes exercises for improving your expression and your presentation. Part 3, "The Art of Performing," considers personal presence and offers exercises for further development of your imagination and intuition in performance. Exercises based on the knowledge gained in part 1 enable you to use your voice with the best possible coordination of mind and body. There is also a chapter on vocal health.

In some cases there are specific references to singing or speaking. However, all discussions, observations, and exercises are pertinent to everyone. The balanced approach that uses physical knowledge, expression, and imagination for healthy voice use and expressive performance is the same for singers and speakers alike.

The book aims to increase awareness so that you can use the principles discussed here to explore ways of understanding your own voice, and the voices of persons with whom you work, and to create your own new exercises based on those principles. Many of the exercises in this book are simple and designed for busy people to do in a short time. They are based on efficient physical and anatomical use. In some cases, however, the exercise is labeled "imaginary" because it is useful in that instance to go beyond real anatomical boundaries in our thinking. In each case, an explanation of an "imaginary" exercise is located in the accompanying text. Some exercises suggest singing. Singing is useful for every voice user! It fine-tunes the voice in ways that no other practice can.

This book features simple, jargon-free language, illustrations with accompanying explanations, observations for you to make, and suggestions for helpful exercises. The aim is to encourage all voice users to think for themselves and share the responsibility of good performance practice and vocal health with their teachers and therapists.

The object of this book is to help its readers value the infinite potential of the human voice and its use in performance, rather than to impose limitations on what might be possible. It is easier to understand what is possible when you have some knowledge of the physical framework and the basic aspects of vocal anatomy and physiology. This will give you a chance to know the vocal instrument better, to realize the practical implications of such knowledge, to develop vocal common sense and healthy voice use, and to perform easily.

The voice and body are full of logic and common sense. Learning to think for yourself, rather than panic about the unknown, is the first step in developing and keeping a healthy voice. Common sense and logic can help release your optimal vocal quality, keep your voice healthy, and allow you then to free your imagination to create compelling performances.

The human voice goes far beyond its purely physical structure. This book encourages you to regard learning about and improving your voice as an unlimited journey with personal fulfillment and vocal satisfaction all along the way. When you want a greater depth of information, you may wish to pursue a more detailed study of anatomy, vocal pedagogy, specific texts on presentation, and the ever-increasing literature on the more esoteric aspects of the voice.

Meribeth Dayme
France, 2005

Acknowledgments

In writing acknowledgments, I always find it difficult to know where to begin. Throughout my life, I have been privileged to meet fascinating teachers, students, and colleagues who have contributed to my knowledge of the voice. From the time I was a child, the only two things that have interested me were singing and how things work. Little did I know that I would eventually combine performance and function.

I began singing and dancing at the age of three and never lost my love affair with song and movement. It was only when I met William Vennard that I began the adventure of really finding out what the whole instrument of the voice meant. It was his dream that teachers of singing would have a much better knowledge of how the body and the voice worked. As I had expressed an interest in knowing more about the body, he surprised me with the announcement that he had managed to enroll me in the anatomy course at the dental school. After that baptism of fire, I was privileged to study and teach both anatomy and singing for many years afterward. Not only had I been privy to many hours of discussion with William Vennard, my teacher and mentor, and Robert Gregg, my anatomy professor; I was able to dissect the body and see for myself the structures that had looked so flat on the page. From there, I was asked to teach in the anatomy lab and later in a program for residents in a hospital. So not only was I finding and discussing the various anatomical structures for 120 students on a daily basis in the lab; I was also invited to observe many surgeries and sit in on doctors' seminars. The awe in which I held the body in the lab became magnified when I saw the living anatomy in surgery. Tissues and structures took on a whole new aspect. At that point, the human body became something wonderful, awesome in its function, its ability to heal itself, and its wisdom.

For me, it was important when I taught anatomy to understand how the students or medical professionals would use it. I wanted it to fit their circumstances. This led to open invitations for me to observe clinics in speech therapy, laryngology, physical therapy, and many kinds of surgery. To be able to have the practical, clinical information alongside teaching and performing has been a superb gift. This knowledge was enhanced, stretched, and even challenged by many years of studying the Alexander technique, the Feldenkrais method, and dance and movement, enjoying a variety of sports, Tai Chi, many other mind-body subjects, and healing methods. Exploring as many things as possible and relating them to vocal performance became for me a mission and a passion.

Singing, teaching singing, and teaching human anatomy led to many wonderful discoveries. Long discussions with my anatomy professors Dr. Robert Gregg and Dr. Ruth Bowden taught me how to look at the body logically and make informed decisions about what was possible. Working with doctors, speech therapists, and physical therapists gave me the scientific appreciation of my art.

I have loved the scientific part of my journey, but I also believe, as has been said, that *science is a good servant and a bad master,* particularly in the world of performance. We need the knowledge and the ability to analyze, but we must not let the analysis interfere with the imagination and the art.

A balanced approach is imperative to understanding the voice and performing well. I met some of the people who helped me develop a scientific/creative balance in London. I had quality time with creative masters like John O'Brien, who taught me so much about movement and the body; Jane Vukovic, a veritable encyclopedia of alternative therapies and systems; and Dadi Janki of the Brahma Kumaris, who taught me what silence and stillness was all about. Years before, when I was working on my Ph.D. in California, my tennis teacher, Louise Brough, encouraged confidence by honoring all my miss hits, or a ball that wasn't perfect in my eyes, by saying to me, "Remember the way you hit that ball; you may want to do it on purpose some day." These are just few of the many people in my life who have been extremely special to my learning.

I am grateful to have this book published by W. W. Norton and for all the help, encouragement, and long conversations with Maribeth Payne, its music editor, and for the dedication of Courtney Fitch, assistant editor, to the production of quality material. Also I must thank Cynthia Vaughn for reading and commenting on the manuscript as well as the feedback from reviewers, who must have spent hours poring over the text and asking valuable questions. Two eyes are never enough when it comes to writing a book. So thank you to everyone from someone who said she would never write or have anything to do with it. What a challenge to the "universe" I issued!

THE

PERFORMER'S VOICE

Introduction

Discovering Your Voice

Simply put, the voice of any performer is a combination of mind, body, imagination, and spirit—all of which work together—no one without the other. This book aims to present a balanced approach to the physical and practical aspects of voice use alongside the aspects of performance that can be improved and enhanced with keen observation and awareness.

Too often we study a subject without considering what is actually possible. This is true of the study of voice many times over. It is easy to become so steeped in tradition and method that we forget to look and hear with an open mind; common sense and obvious information that could be gained from a greater awareness escapes our notice. Although it is useful to gain inspiration from past knowledge, it is at the same time important not to let it blind and deafen us to the new discoveries we can make.

Students in the performing arts have a long history of learning by rote (studying one method and then passing on the information as they have remembered it). When this happens, it becomes scary for them to go beyond traditional thinking or to return to some basic concepts that have been overlooked over time. Old, outdated knowledge about vocal function is still prevalent in the artistic and medical communities, and the public at large, but our awareness is changing and evolving with the current research and understanding about the body and the function of the voice. Even though voice research has come a long way, it remains in its infancy. New "scientific" knowledge is indeed helpful, but we must maintain the goal of balance in performance— not just an intellectual knowledge of how the voice works.

Professionals in the field of voice and their students are today expected to attain a basic knowledge of their instrument and how it works. This can seem a daunting task to those who choose the performing arts rather than science as a calling. Yet, increasingly the distinctions between art and science are blurred; meetings and seminars include speakers from all areas of voice-related study—doctors, therapists, actors, singers, sports physiologists, Alexander and Feldenkrais teachers, and many others. This is an exciting time of learning from one another. To be comfortable with this convergence of knowledge, performers and their teachers now, more than ever, need a solid core of information about healthy and effective vocal use and performance. All voice professions benefit by being able to talk to one another and to be comfortable with the language of each area.

DISCOVER MORE ABOUT YOUR VOICE

Become a "people watcher." Functional knowledge of anatomy derives from studying people as well as texts. Do your best to observe the human body as if you were a curious newcomer without preconceived ideas or assumptions. It is too easy for performers and voice professionals to get caught up in the myths of voice use rather than to see the reality.

A quiet mind is a real asset to your observations and awareness. An analytical mind running at full speed is not generally compatible with good observation. Being mentally quiet while observing leads to spontaneous, creative, and intuitive responses. Curiosity and "quiet being" during observation can be your greatest gift to yourself.

Studying how singers and speakers use their bodies and voices is a fascinating and delightful adventure. Each person needs to be seen as a three-dimensional sculpture. Too often, voice teachers view their students only from the front and miss all the information to be gained by looking from the sides and the back. Sometimes doctors tend to examine the throat and vocal folds from the inside and forget to notice external physical characteristics of their patients that also might be contributing to a vocal problem. Individual patterns are unique, and you will find that with keen observation you will become better at devising specific strategies to help yourself and possibly others. As a teacher of the vocal arts, ask yourself, "Am I teaching voice to the student, or teaching the student, voice?" If the answer is the latter, then observing how each individual functions physically and reacts to your instructions is crucial to teaching success.

The physical act of making sound begins with the thought of producing that sound. Ideally, the body responds by becoming filled with a dynamic and flexible energy. This creates a receptive, vibrant instrument and the space for efficient breathing and sound production. When it takes excessive energy or work to create sound, unneeded muscles begin to "help," causing the body to become tense and inflexible rather than a responsive instrument. When muscles contract, the body shrinks; when they relax, the body expands. You can never become expansive through muscle contraction; expansion is a letting go. Notice when a singer or speaker is shrinking, rather than expanding, to make sound. Some performers look an inch shorter by the time they finish their selection. This can be one of the most important observations you will ever make. Shrinking inhibits good voice quality, and expanding enhances it.

BEGINNING TO LEARN ABOUT THE VOICE

You can learn many things about the voice just by close observations, or by general study of the body and its anatomical structure. Here are some suggestions to get you started.

1. Use a mirror or a video camera to observe yourself. Treat yourself as if you were seeing a stranger perform. Look for habits that interfere with your voice use and communication. Observe performers at every opportunity. Which ones communicate with you best? What are the positive characteristics they exhibit?

2. Observe people in the street, in buses, and in stores. How are they maintaining their physical balance? Are they in balance because of excellent alignment? Or are they in balance because the imbalances counteract one another?

3. Human "anatomy books" are all around you. Look at each anatomical area of the body in the context of the whole picture. How is each area affected by the adjacent structures? For example, is the jaw being affected by lip movement, or vice versa? Is the position of the head affecting the shoulders and chest in any way?

4. Learn the names of the bones of the body. It is much easier to be sensible and logical about muscle movement when you know the name of the bone or cartilage to which it attaches (see figure I.1).

5. Make your own models and drawings wherever possible, and imagine in three dimensions whenever you see an illustration. Since the body is multidimensional, using models is

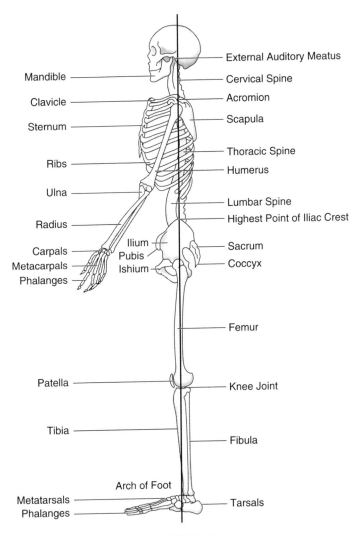

External Auditory Meatus

Mandible

Cervical Spine

Clavicle

Acromion

Sternum

Scapula

Thoracic Spine

Ribs

Humerus

Ulna

Lumbar Spine

Radius

Highest Point of Iliac Crest

Carpals

Ilium

Sacrum

Pubis

Metacarpals

Coccyx

Ishium

Phalanges

Femur

Patella

Knee Joint

Tibia

Fibula

Arch of Foot

Metatarsals

Tarsals

Phalanges

FIGURE I.1
Bones of the skeleton

more useful than looking at flat drawings to most people. The more elements in the drawings, the more difficult they are to understand. Poring over an illustration without having seen the real structure demands a lot of the reader.

6. Appreciate the innate wisdom of the human body that gets us through life without having to know everything that is going on inside it.

7. Be adventurous and read journals and articles devoted to the voice. If you are new to reading scientific materials, first get an overview by reading the abstract and the introduction. Next read the conclusion. After reading these, you will probably know whether you want to read the rest. This approach will keep you from wasting energy on articles that are irrelevant to your interest.

ASSESSING A VOICE: LOOKING, LISTENING, AND PERCEIVING

Whether you are working with your own voice or with someone else's, it is wise to have a practical way of looking and listening. Many voice professionals use far too many muscles and unnecessary energy to speak or sing. Using too much effort, or more muscles than necessary, to perform an action is called muscular accommodation. It causes and contributes to most vocal problems, even though some people are able to speak or sing with an acceptable quality (to the audience) in spite of their physical misuse.

Communication calls for a balance of what is seen, what is heard, and what is perceived. The evaluator must be able to look, listen, and sense with accuracy. What follows are some guidelines for assessment of a professional voice.

Guidelines for Voice Assessment

Here are things to look for, to listen for, and to perceive when you evaluate a voice. Just observe; do not interrupt yourself with judgments as to right or wrong, because you cannot see when you are busy judging. You can use these guidelines by training a video camera on yourself, to evaluate a friend or colleague, or to ask a colleague or teacher to assess your voice use.

Looking

Look for the following:

1. General patterns
   - The general energy of the performer (Is she nervous? calm? too relaxed?)
   - Eyes that see and are fully present
   - Physical and mental presence
   - Awareness of differences in physical sensation when asked to make changes
2. Alignment patterns
   - Sagging or distension of the body, either sideways, front to back, or in the chest or abdomen
   - Exaggerated curves of the back
   - Locking of the back
   - Scoliosis (S curve in the back) or a tendency to sag into one side
   - One hip higher than the other
   - Locked knees
   - A head level or straight on the shoulders
   - The head in relationship to the shoulders (Is it poked forward, pulled down, or leaning to the right or left?)

3. Physical patterns
   - Physical freedom of the head, neck, torso, hips, and legs
   - Stiff or relaxed in action and movement
   - Movements that are symmetrical or misaligned
   - Movements that seem withheld, jerky, or pulled downward
   - Tension in the legs or feet when standing or sitting
   - Deviation of the jaw from the midline during speech or singing
   - Excessive or forced movement of the jaw
   - Exaggeration or distortion of the lips
   - Brows that are wrinkled or have worried look
   - Eyes—patterns of seeing, staring, or looking up
4. Breathing patterns
   - Breathing that is easy or labored
   - Excessive or natural-looking inhalation
   - Shoulder movement when inhaling
   - Downward movement of the upper chest when making sound
   - Expansion of the chest or back
   - Ribs held out in a rigid manner
   - A breathing pattern that is high, wide, or long
   - Excessive distension of the abdomen on inhalation or exhalation
   - Evidence of excessive pressure because of overbreathing or holding the breath

Listening

Listen for the following audible patterns:

- Clarity, distortion, or muffling of sound
- A pleasant or unpleasant quality
- Gasping for air during speaking or singing
- Excess breath in the sound
- Excess tension in the sound
- Differences in the speaking and singing voice, or the speaking and acting voice

Perceiving

Watch for possible misconceptions:

- The performer's perceptions about what he/she is doing
- Understanding of how sound is made
- Understanding of voice type (For example, is a mezzo-soprano trying to sound full and deep when her voice is that way already?)
- Trying to sound more powerful or important by creating excess tension in the throat

AWARENESS

Awareness begins with educated observation. Not only will you see what is creating a problem or a vocal obstacle for others; you will also begin to sense your own balance or lack of it. Soon you will be able to see and hear vocal efficiency. Performers have often accused good teachers of having eyes in the backs of their heads. That is because the teachers have seen the problem and heard the results so often that they can easily identify the issue

in more ways than one. However, your own awareness and observation will enable you to create systematic ways of correcting
yourself without unnecessary panic. The benefit will be a different, and more equal, relationship with your voice teachers and
coaches, voice therapists, doctors, and colleagues in the performing arts.

USING THIS BOOK

The best way to use this book is to follow your curiosity and find
what suits your needs. Each section contains very different material. If you do not want to read about the vocal anatomy, begin
with the section on performance, or search out the observations
and exercise boxes in each section. These are practical and can
stand on their own merit. Ultimately, *The Performer's Voice* is
intended to help you enjoy and enhance your vocal path.

PART I

Making Sense
of Vocal Mechanics

Most nonvocal performers know quite a lot about their instruments. They have a distinct advantage in that they can take them apart, look at them, modify various aspects, and, in general, see them objectively. The same is not true, however, for the human voice. It lives inside a whole person and is highly influenced by what is going on in that person.

The body and the voice it contains are both magical, and both are best viewed with curiosity and excitement rather than as mysterious, scary objects. What happens in and to your body directly affects your voice; the two are intertwined. It is impossible to study the voice without looking at the body.

The entire body is your instrument, and it "sings" and vibrates with all of its molecular structure. The voice is vibration also; and by using your voice with a coordinated integration of the whole body, you are literally "singing yourself." The voice functions best when it is treated as part of the whole rather than isolated. A student attending my vocal anatomy course was very disappointed to find out that singers have no special anatomical structure that makes them singers. The whole body instrument is special, and everybody has one. There are obvious patterns and structures in the body that can be understood without a degree in science or metaphysics. Part I is dedicated to helping you understand your instrument better.

1

The Logic and Wisdom
of the Body

Most voice professionals are expected to know something about their instrument; many books about the voice thus include some anatomy and physiology. As was mentioned earlier, this idea can panic performers and their teachers. In this book the chapters on vocal function are meant to eliminate some of the panic and to begin the process of exploring and enjoying just how the body and voice work. What performers want is *vocal common sense*. The information that follows helps you acquire that.

To begin very simply, we have a framework of bones that are held together by strong ligaments and membranes and moved by means of muscles. In addition, every structure in the body comes gift-wrapped with a thin, filmy glistening covering called connective tissue, or fascia, which surrounds everything in the body. A command center (the central nervous system) receives information and deals with it—sometimes without our knowing, and at other times to make us conscious of a need to adjust something, whether it is physical or mental.

THE SKELETAL STRUCTURE

Every living organism has some sort of skeletal structure. The human skeleton can be compared to the scaffolding of a building. It is crucial to the stability of your "house." The balance and alignment of the skeleton are directly related to the healthy functioning of joints, muscles, organs, and especially the voice. Whenever you participate in some kind of intense activity out of alignment, every muscle in your body has to adjust to keep you balanced. Over time, if this activity becomes a habit, these adjusted muscles pull on their bony attachments and can displace the bones. Poor alignment takes away the body's ability to respond spontaneously and forces the brain to override the subconscious system.

When there is lack of attention to efficient physical alignment, people have to override their natural subconscious system and to work hard to overcome the "crooked framework." They are then presented with techniques that necessitate overly conscious attention to the physical activity that is being studied—whether it is sport, dance, or voice use.

The tissues associated with the skeletal joints include ligaments, which are very strong; membranes, which are less strong, and surround the joint; and tendons from muscles. The strong ligaments that stabilize and hold the skeleton together help maintain the integrity of joint alignment. They cannot cause movement. Membranes are less strong and furnish a kind of binding for joints. Those membranes surrounding a joint have cells that manufacture and provide lubrication for that joint. Tendons are associated with muscle and serve to attach the muscle to bone. They are not primarily a joint tissue but can contribute to the stability of the joint when the muscles are strengthened. All of these tissues have minimal elasticity and a poor blood supply (unlike muscles, which are richly endowed with blood). When you tear or injure them, they are therefore slow to heal.

When you look at a skeleton more closely, you can understand the possibilities of movement of a particular joint by observing the shapes of both of the bones or cartilages that touch to form the joint. For example, at the hip joint, the thigh bone (femur) has a rounded end that fits into a socket in the hip (see figure 1.1). This shape allows the femur to move in a variety of ways according to the restrictions of the hip socket. On first glance, it might appear that the leg can make complete circles. However, you know that your leg will not do that. The restriction here lies not in the structure of the bones but in strong ligaments that stabilize the joint. Other joints, such as the elbow, have very definite joint restriction. This is obvious when you notice how the ulna bone of the forearm fits into the humerus. It makes sense— you would not want to be able to bend your elbow both ways, for it would do very strange things to the shape and muscles of your forearm.

Every joint is different and must be observed closely. This is also true of the joints in the larynx. If you really wish to under-

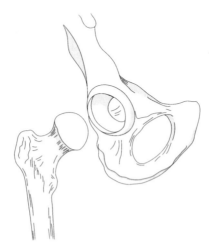

FIGURE 1.1
Hip joint

stand vocal muscle movement and potential, begin by learning all you can about the joints. You will then be able to make logical deductions regarding the actions of that joint and the positions of the muscles that move it. Trying to memorize muscle names without some basis for logical understanding can lead to confusion and misinformation.

HOW MUSCLES WORK

There are several types of muscle, including skeletal (or striated), cardiac (specific to the heart), and smooth (found around organs, arteries, and veins). We will discuss only skeletal muscle, because this is the type that causes the body to move. (These have also been called voluntary muscles.) Knowing the names of muscles is helpful, but knowing how they work and where they attach is the way to make sense of their action.

Muscles shortening across joints cause the body to move. They contract by a message from the nervous system and relax when that message stops. Conscious movement begins with a signal from the brain. This message is much like a tiny electric stimulus (see figures 1.2a and 1.2b). This electrochemical stimulus causes the muscle fibers to shorten and appear bulkier. When the message from the brain stops, the contraction stops and the muscles relax. Once a movement is practiced enough, it is remembered by the brain and becomes subconscious and spontaneous. That is why we practice and why careful practice is important. You do not want your brain to remember unhelpful messages; it takes too much time to unlearn the bad habit.

The brain not only remembers bad habits but sometimes fails to shut off. When people carry constant tension (meaning continual messages to the muscles to contract), the muscles get no complete release and the person does not truly relax. The tense

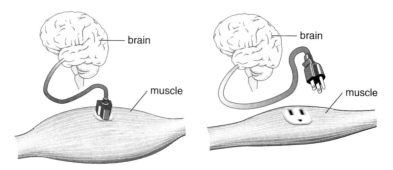

FIGURE 1.2a
Muscle contraction

FIGURE 1.2b
Muscle release

person is diverting a lot of energy away from the physical act he or she wishes to perform, whether it is singing, speaking, acting, or sport.

In order for any joint movement to occur, a muscle must contract. For example, bend your elbow. The muscle that does that is the biceps. When it contracts, its attachments at the front of your upper arm (humerus), and part of the forearm (radius), near the elbow, cause the elbow to bend. Should you now wish to straighten your arm, the muscle at the back of your arm (triceps) contracts and the muscles at the front relax. Those muscles on opposite sides of a bone usually have opposing actions and are called antagonists. Normally, one muscle will release as the other one contracts. When both sides contract at the same time, they stabilize the elbow joint. There are times when you want a stable joint and muscles working together. Though such stabilization is needed on occasion, as in the hip when standing on one leg, at other times too many muscles working at once decreases flexibility and ability to respond. When you want maximum joint movement, one muscle must be able to contract without antagonism from the muscle on the opposite side. This kind of muscular tug of war can happen in the throat and larynx as well—only it is much more complicated there.

Muscles are generally named for their shape, their location in the body, the place of their attachment, or their function. It is helpful to know that when you see a muscle that has *superior* as part of its name, you can be sure that there is an *inferior* one as well. Sometimes there is also a *middle* muscle, as in the three constrictors of the pharynx—superior, middle, and inferior. Likewise, when a muscle is labeled *major,* there is a *minor* by the same name.

The origins, insertions, and direction of the muscle fibers will show you the direction of the action. It is generally true, but not always, that the origin of a muscle is the most stable and the insertion the more mobile. For example, the pectoralis major muscle of the chest originates along the edge of the sternum and first eight ribs and inserts on the humerus. Obviously the humerus is more likely to move than the chest.

The same muscle cannot perform two different actions. For instance, the muscle that moves the vocal folds apart cannot also move them together. This knowledge will help you when you look at anatomical pictures and try to decide what the muscle might do.

ANATOMICAL TERMINOLOGY

As you gain confidence with a basic understanding of the body, you may wish to look at anatomy textbooks. Designed for medical students and allied professions, they are probably too detailed for most performers. However, you may want to know more. If so, stick to the information you want to find rather than get lost in all the detail. For example, if you want to learn more about a muscle and its action, be very focused in your approach. Ignore the parts about blood supply, nerves, and the lymph system. Too much information can boggle the mind and confuse the issue. However, one thing you do need to know—that is, how anatomical terminology is derived.

All anatomy books use *anatomical position* as their point of reference for describing the body. This universal reference ensures a uniform description of where structures are located. When a person is standing, anatomical position is shown with eyes, head, and toes directed forward and the upper limbs hanging by the sides with the palms facing forward (see figure 1.3). Note that this means the forearms and palms are considered to be the front (or anterior).

Anatomical terminology is very specific. Consistency of description is essential in the world of science; otherwise no one could share research or medical-surgical techniques. The possibility of duplicating research exactly is important for validating it. If you wish to pursue your vocal anatomy further, learn something about the terminology so that you can find what you need in anatomy books. A summary of anatomical terminology can be found in appendix A of this book.

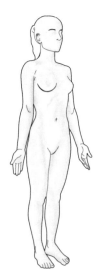

FIGURE 1.3
Anatomical position

A BRIEF OVERVIEW
OF THE NERVOUS SYSTEM

The nervous system is like a massive telephone exchange that is full of outgoing and incoming messages. The central nervous system consists of the brain and the spinal cord. The peripheral nervous system (sometimes referred to as the voluntary system) is an extension of the brain and spinal chord and acts as the messenger, sending information from the brain to the periphery, and from the skin and muscles back to the brain.

Every time you want to move, your brain sends a message to the appropriate muscles to do the job. Think about moving a very heavy object. Knowing that the object is heavy, you send the message to your brain that a lot of muscle power will be needed. You then get what you need. Think also of perceiving something to be heavy when it is really light. You have told your brain that you need a lot of power and you are given that energy, only to find out that you are lifting something light, and then it nearly flies over your head. Your perceptions can give your brain misinformation, but your body will follow your mental orders. This is a good reason not to have too many misinformed perceptions.

There is an autonomic nervous system (sometimes called the involuntary system), consisting of the sympathetic and parasympathetic nerves. The sympathetic nerves are responsible for the adrenaline rush people get. They form what is often called the "flight or fright system." The parasympathetic nerves help maintain calm, normality, digestion, and general organ function. When we have too much nervous energy, the sympathetic nerves are stimulated too often and can drain our reserves of adrenaline. So down time and relaxation are essential for performers, who tend to live on adrenaline much of the time.

The messages to the central nervous system come from special cells in the skin that register touch, heat, cold, and pain. These cells are constantly sending information to the central nervous system for evaluation and action if needed. Interestingly, the vocal folds have few pain fibers. That is one reason why people do not get the message of vocal abuse early enough.

TENSION AND ANXIETY

Anxiety is a fact of life for most performers. The more experienced they are, the more confident they usually are, and therefore the better able to control their nerves. However, there is a tendency for performers to be overly self-critical and prone to excess anxiety, and the excessive adrenaline leads to inefficient physical coordination. Excess tension can occur regardless of nervousness and is the result of too much muscular effort. In either case, the performance is compromised.

Visualization (see chapter 11) is a useful tool for anyone appearing onstage. As was stated earlier, the nervous system reacts to your perceptions and pictures. Picturing yourself performing comfortably, knowing the music and/or text, and enjoying what you are doing is therefore one very effective way to balance the nerves. It makes your nervous system think you have done it before and allows you to be more confident.

ENJOY BEING AN INFORMED PERFORMER

Making sense of the body is almost easier for persons who know nothing about it than for those who have studied it as part of their training. Because the typical education in anatomy demands a lot of memorization, persons who can look at it with unprejudiced eyes may understand it in a more functional way. Curiosity about the body comes naturally for most people and leads them to want to know more.

Study of vocal anatomy can bring a lot of pleasure and answers to many questions, but also frustration because we don't know all the answers. No one does. How each person will respond both physically and mentally can be very different. Looking as logically as possible while leaving space for new information is therefore an important criterion for seeing and hearing what is happening when people use their voices.

2

Physical Alignment
and Balance

Physical alignment (or posture) contributes to your balance, ease of movement, sense of well-being, health, energy, ease of breathing, and efficient voice production, as well as to how others perceive you. For anyone associated with the vocal arts, the importance of understanding and modeling good physical alignment and balance can hardly be overstated. Resolution of problems of alignment and posture can lead to startling improvement in voice production.

Posture is dynamic; that is, all of the cells of the body are full of vibrating atoms that we cannot see. These cells need space in which to move. When alignment is poor and muscles are tight, cells, organs, and joints cannot function efficiently. Thus, rather than being expansive and free, the body shrinks, making it difficult to move, breathe easily, or engage in physical activity without danger of injury.

USING THE WHOLE BODY

When we think of the body as a mass of vibrating atoms, each one of which needs space to move, we understand that by expanding (releasing appropriate muscles) physically we contribute to a much more efficient posture. Any specific area of the body that shrinks unnecessarily in order to perform its function will be working against itself, "cramping" part of the vibration, creating excess tension, and changing the vocal quality in the process. Vocal artists are best able to "sound" with their whole body when there is no excess tension and there is a dynamic physical ease. This is vital to the performer who wants to achieve optimal tone quality.

PHYSICAL AWARENESS

Physical awareness comes from sensory feedback; it is neither a verbal exercise nor an intellectual one. People stand and move according to their perceptions of good posture, and giving verbal directions will generally confuse the issue. Posture is kinesthetic and is best corrected by means of touch to give new directions to muscles, and accurate descriptions of efficient physical alignment to create new perceptions. There are some strange-looking people wandering about who have been given verbal postural corrections. Professionals in, and those working with, the vocal arts need to know how good alignment feels and looks. For this reason it is wise for persons involved with the voice to have lessons in the Alexander technique, the Feldenkrais method, or similar mind-body awareness techniques (at least ten lessons are recommended). Unless you feel these changes for yourself, you cannot describe them or relay the information adequately.

Physical Awareness

Becoming aware of one's own body is the key to change and making new choices. When we do not know how, or whether, we are balanced, it is difficult to see the need for change—even when told by someone else. For these observations, first feel the answers to the questions, then use a mirror, video feedback, or a partner or teacher.

Stand or sit quietly and become aware of your body. Allow your attention to feel any patterns of tension or unbalance. Sometimes just becoming aware of these areas will enable you to make minor corrections for yourself.

1. Look for imbalance in the body. Is one shoulder higher than the other? Is one arm held higher or more tensely than the other?
2. Is the head to one side?
3. Are the shoulders pulled in, back, concave?
4. What are the eyes doing? Looking ahead and "seeing" or not here?
5. Are the knees locked when standing?
6. Are the feet evenly in contact with the floor, with the weight equally balanced on both feet?
7. What happens to the body when you are singing or speaking? Do you change your balance in any way? Do your face, eyes, mouth, neck, or shoulders become distorted or asymmetrical? Is the body rigid or dynamic?
8. How does vocal quality change when posture is changed or corrected? How does the breathing pattern change?

BALANCED ALIGNMENT

It is easy to confuse what is habitual with what is natural. "Natural" is that which the body can do reflexively and ideally. "Habitual" is everything we have done over years of repeated use to create current physical shapes and patterns. Habits can be changed.

Efficient alignment has been defined by researchers in medical biomechanics, teachers of Alexander technique, and experts in other fields pertaining to efficient physical balance. They are in relative agreement about what constitutes an efficient alignment. It can be described as follows:

FIGURE 2.1
Balanced alignment
Note: The easiest way for you to see this for yourself is to line up with the edge of a door or something that is straight and use a video to film the result.

A line dropped from the top of the head will fall through the ear, the point of the shoulder (where the clavicle touches the acromion of the scapula), the highest point of the pelvis, just behind the kneecap and just in front of the ankle (see figure 2.1).

Such an alignment allows the body to be well balanced with gravitational forces, to look and feel lighter and taller, and to move easily. When sitting, one maintains the same integrity of the crown of the head to the pelvis. Shoulders go *out*, not back. Efforts to pull them backward result in neck and back tension and send the head forward; pulling them forward cramps the chest and inhibits breathing. When the head is forward of the shoulders, the muscles between the head and shoulders protect you by contracting to hold your head in place. The result is aching shoulder muscles and a body badly pulled out of balance. You can check this by protruding your head and then feeling your shoulder muscles. They will be very tight and inflexible. When the head is aligned properly, the shoulder muscles let go and feel more pliable to the touch. The body is then more balanced with gravity and can be used without undue extra muscular tension.

When we change our postural habits, we create a period of physical confusion. We have programmed our bodies in certain ways, and when these patterns are altered we feel strange. For example, if you tend to slump, your back will be rounded, causing the back muscles to stretch and your chest and abdomen to collapse. When you return to a balanced posture, the back muscles will be working efficiently and the front muscles will be more stretched. All of this new muscular activity may make you think you feel stiff or tight. Stay with it, and allow your body to adopt a new balance. Just make sure you are not trying to hold on to or fix the new alignment, but are at ease. Always remember that you are dynamic, not static.

Establishing Efficient Alignment and Improving Your Posture

Here are a variety of exercises for establishing and improving your posture, and experimenting with sound in different alignments. Become used to the feeling of being aligned in your everyday life, and it will become a good performance habit with little effort.

Establishing a Good Alignment
The principles in these exercises are essential in standing or sitting.

1. *Make sure your feet are fully on the floor.* Feeling secure and grounded is important. Feel every pore of the sole of your feet touching the floor. It may help to imagine that your feet are Velcroed to the ground—even if you are wearing elevated shoes or high heels. When you imagine that your feet are fully on the ground, you can shift your weight forward from the ankles (when necessary) without the heels' lifting.

2. *Feel as though the crown (not the top) of your head is growing upward.* This will lengthen the back of your neck and help you feel your spine lengthening as well. It is here that most people attempt to get this stretch by lifting the chin. Lifting the chin only shortens the back of the neck and causes you to have to look down your nose to see people (see figure 2.2).

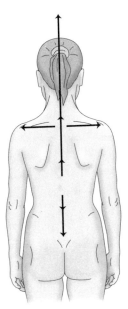

FIGURE 2.2
Imagery for lengthening the spine (back view)

3. *Make sure your knees are slightly loose and able to bend if necessary.* One poor habit that affects posture is that of locked knees. You can experiment with this. Notice that when you lock your knees and push back on them, the bottom becomes elevated and causes the lower back to arch—not a look that excites many people.

4. *Last, balance your weight evenly between the balls of the feet and heels.* When your feet feel secure on the floor, you can change the balance by moving your whole body from your ankles. You can test your balance by rising on your toes. Ideally, you will be able to rise on your toes by pushing through the feet. Many people try to shift forward by leading with the pelvis or head. If you have to move forward to rise up, your weight has been too far back. Most people are shocked to find out how far backward or forward they have been standing habitually.

Remember to breathe. For some reason, people tend to hold their breath when concentrating on posture.

Most likely you will be using your muscles a little differently when you correct your alignment. You may feel strange, even stiff, because your body is more stretched. However, a video camera or partner can confirm that you do not look weird and thereby allay your fears.

Improving Your Posture

1. Grab yourself by the nape of the neck, and pull your head up with your hand. Ideally you will feel your spine begin to lengthen and your upper back begin to stretch.

2. Think of yourself as expanding in every direction to fill any doorway you enter.

⤳ Remember you are a dynamic entity, full of vibration. At no time do you want to look like a robot.

Exploring Sound Quality through Posture

You can do these exercises with a partner or by filming yourself on video. Sustain a sound, sing or speak a phrase while doing the exercises below.

1. Change the position of your head, first forward, then with chin pulled into chest, then in a normal position with ears over shoulders. Note the difference in quality with each change.

2. Alter your balance first by shifting your weight onto your heels, then too far forward, and last to a balanced position. Notice that when your weight is too far back, the back muscles have to work very hard and the knees tend to lock. It takes a lot of extra muscular effort to keep yourself in that position and takes away from the efficiency of singing or speaking.

3. Experiment with a number a ways of altering your body position, and note the changes in sound. How does each new posture affect sound quality?

4. Let your abdomen go completely slack, then look at your back in a mirror. Usually this action creates an overly curved lower back and can make it difficult to stand or breathe properly.

Using a Model to Find Out How You Look

This three-person exercise enables you to see and describe your personal alignment. Do it two times, once standing and once sitting. It is easier if your model is standing or sitting beside you rather than in front.

1. Stand and sit in your habitual posture.
2. Ask a friend to stand and sit exactly like you.
3. Ask a third person to make sure that the friend is copying you accurately.
4. Have the friend describe how it feels to be in your alignment.
5. Now move around your friend to see how *you* look.

BALANCE IN PERFORMANCE

Many performers and voice professionals regard physical balance as important, but they often assume they are fully aware of their posture when in fact they are not. In their eagerness to communicate, and in the heat of performance, this balance is often the first thing to go. By being very aware of your alignment in your practice and rehearsals, you will be able to perceive when you are uncomfortable or when something seems to be missing vocally. Create a checklist of possible causes. Poor alignment is one that may well be at the top of the list. Careful attention to posture during practice will instill good habits that remain during performance. This will allow you to perform well without sabotaging your vocal quality and message.

3

Breathing

Breathing is a reflex action that occurs approximately 24,400 times a day. The efficiency of this act can be altered by posture, poor physical habits, exercise, injury, air quality, and even misconceptions about how we breathe. For maximum respiratory efficiency, the body must be in good physical balance. This means that the air supply (lungs), vibrator (larynx), and resonator (pharynx) are aligned and in the optimal position for efficient breathing. To discuss breathing without first looking at and/or correcting posture is therefore to create problems rather than to solve them.

Vocal artists need an unimpeded face, neck, and larynx. If the breathing pattern involves use of neck muscles, high shoulders, or gulping of air with the mouth, it will be very difficult for the voice to function well or easily. Poor breathing patterns are found most often in pop singers and women speakers. Their high-chested breathing contributes to vocal tension and strident vocal qualities.

THE ANATOMICAL BASIS OF BREATHING

The vocal arts are fraught with differing perceptions of how the act of breathing occurs. The best way to learn about breathing is to forget everything you know about it, for a moment, and first study the anatomical description of respiration. It will help you form a basis for objective observation, rather than a dependency on hearsay and descriptions altered to *fit* the process of singing and dramatic voice use.

The most basic pattern we have for breathing is the one that is a subconscious reflex, *passive* respiration. All other healthy patterns are versions of passive respiration with more muscle added, according to the activity. Below is a description of the basic pattern, which involves minimal muscle action except for the diaphragm.

- The physiological need for oxygen is monitored by the brain, which sends a message to the diaphragm.
- The diaphragm contracts (moves down), thus enlarging the area in the chest that includes the highly mobile lower ribs (creating expansion in the abdomen if it is not held tightly).
- The enlargement of the chest stretches the elastic tissues of the lungs and trachea; the ensuing vacuum-like situation creates an air pressure lower than that of the surrounding atmosphere, and air is drawn inward.
- During expiration the diaphragm returns to a relaxed position, and the stretched elastic tissues and rib cage return to a pre-inspiration state.

The cycle repeats itself again and again according to the balance of oxygen and carbon dioxide in the body. This balance helps to maintain the general physiological well-being of the body, a state known as homeostasis.

When more breath and power are needed—as in physical exercise, singing, or dramatic voice use—more muscles are needed to help increase the volume of air. With good alignment, however, comes more efficient use of air, and you may require less energy than you think.

BREATHING FOR PERFORMERS

In an easily produced voice, the inspired air passes *silently* through a spacious, free throat and widely separated vocal folds, into a chest in which the upper part is stable, not rigid, and the back and lower portions are flexible enough to permit lateral and posterior expansion of the ribs. At the same time, the abdominal muscles need to be relaxed enough to allow the downward excursion of the diaphragm. During expiration there is a recoil of the elastic tissues of the lungs and trachea, balanced and slowed by a combination of maintaining good posture and actively contracting the lower muscles of the abdomen. This action sets up a balance of pressures in the abdomen, in the chest, and at the level of the larynx that ultimately helps the performer maintain a steady air pressure. When the head, shoulders, and hips are aligned, the breathing mechanism performs these actions with minimal energy and without muscular compensation or physical or vocal distortion.

One possible reason for the multiple theories of breathing for vocal artists is that they do not adequately correct their posture before improving their breathing. For example, many people have excessive tension in the lower back, which immobilizes the lower ribs. This means that any action of the diaphragm then has to move the abdomen, creating an excessive frontal displacement with the action of the breath. When enough performers breathe in this manner, it makes people consider it normal and it then becomes a teaching method.

Observing Patterns of Breathing and
Their Effects on Performance

Breath is a necessity of life, and people will take in air any way they can. You can observe many different ways that people breathe. Some of these are efficient for good vocal function, and some are not. Observe the following without judging the merit of them at the moment.

1. Note the breathing patterns of different people when they talk or sing. Do they gulp or gasp for air? Do they use the ribs in the back at all? Do they look like an accordion with a lot of movement up and down at the level of the waist?

2. What happens to your breathing pattern when your knees are stiff or locked? You may notice that the lower back locks as well.

3. Observe and feel your own breathing patterns. Experiment with ideas you have experienced, read about in books on vocal technique, or observed in other performers. What happens when you hold your abdomen in tightly and try to take a deep breath? What area will move instead? Explore and find out for yourself what works.

4. What happens to the breath when you march, walk, or lightly run while singing or speaking? You may find you breathe without thinking and have enough air. When the body is otherwise engaged, breathing will happen reflexively.

5. Observe what happens to the breath when you stand *still* to sing. For many people, still means a stoppage of all movement, including breath. The tendency is to begin to "control" the breath by means of tension rather than elastic, full-body alignment. The challenge is to stand

without becoming fixed or rigid and to remem
the body is living and dynamic.

There are two simple observations about breath; it comes in,
and it goes out. Logically, for the breath to enter the lungs the
volume of the chest must enlarge; for air to leave the lungs, the
volume must get smaller. Where must muscles be placed to
expand the volume of the chest? And where must they be placed
to make it smaller? When you can answer these questions, you
know quite a lot about breathing.

Examine the skeleton in figure 3.1. The structure of the rib
cage gives many clues about its possible movement. The close-
ness of the thoracic vertebrae and the attachment of the ribs to
the sternum limit the movement of all but the lowest five ribs.
The biggest space available for expansion is the bottom of the
rib cage.

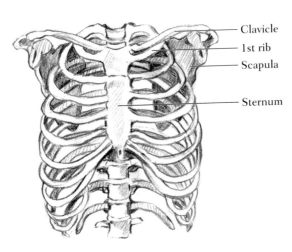

Clavicle
1st rib
Scapula

Sternum

FIGURE 3.1
Structure of the rib cage

THE SKELETAL FRAMEWORK OF BREATHING

You could claim that the whole body provides the framework for breathing. However, the main framework for breathing consists of the skull and mandible, clavicle, scapula, sternum, ribs, spine, and pelvis. Notice that the first seven ribs attach directly to the sternum. This will limit the possibilities of their movement to up and down rather than outward. Ribs 8–10 are attached indirectly to the sternum and have much more lateral mobility. Thus, anatomy texts often describe these movements as "pump handle" and "bucket handle," respectively. The two lowest ribs (11–12) have no anterior attachments and are called floating ribs. The posterior portion of the diaphragm and the deep muscles of the back that attach to the pelvis and lower ribs maintain the stability of these ribs.

INHALATION

The most important muscle in inspiration is the diaphragm. It occupies the bottom of the rib cage. It roughly resembles a large, unusually shaped hat that fits high into the rib cage (see figures 3.2a and 3.2b). It is attached to the lowest ribs at the back, the spine, all around the lower borders of the rib cage, and the lowest part of the breastbone. The diaphragm is highest in the front and has the most muscle fibers at the sides and back. When the diaphragm contracts, it moves down, causing ribs 8–10 to move outward and to pull the elastic lung tissue with them. The dimension of the rib cage is increased, and a negative air pressure is created inside the chest. The lungs are related to the diaphragm and ribs by covering layers of pleura that slide on each other. Normally, there is a vacuum between the two layers, and this causes the lungs to move with the ribs and diaphragm.

FIGURE 3.2a
Diaphragm as a "hat"

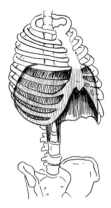

FIGURE 3.2b
Position of diaphragm in rib cage

The diaphragm never loses its dome shape and becomes completely flat, nor can it become inverted. It can move down about 2.5 inches at most. There is little movement in the front, since the vast majority of the muscle fibers are at the sides and back.

Other important muscles that increase the space in the rib cage are located deep in the back, and attach to the bony processes (parts of a bone that stick out) on the sides of the thoracic vertebra and the ribs immediately below. These attachments give these muscles the leverage to raise the ribs slightly and swing them outward. These muscles are called the levatores costarum (see figure 3.3).

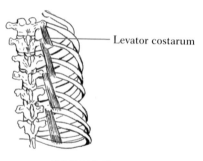

FIGURE 3.3
Levator costarum muscles

Exercises for Easy Inhalation

These exercises are designed to help you get the feeling of breathing low and deep and to get the back ribs active. Once you have the physical feeling, then sing or speak. It is important to feel these movements as you make sound.

For Freedom and Feeling Movement in the Lower Ribs at the Back

1. Sit in a chair with both feet on the floor, and allow your body to fold onto your thighs, your arms to hang freely, and your head to flop down so that the top of your head is pointing toward the floor. Now take a big breath, making sure that the shoulders are not involved. You will find that the back ribs respond because the pressure of your body weight over your thighs prevents excessive movement of the abdomen.

2. While sitting in a chair, feel your in-breath move your back into the chair.

3. Standing in good alignment, place the backs of your hands (palms facing out) on the lower back ribs (see figure 3.4). As you breathe in, feel your breath expand the

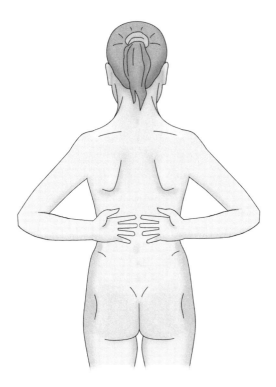

FIGURE 3.4
Placement of hands on lower ribs
Note: Palms are facing away from the body

back ribs so that they push your hands backward. If your back has been locked, you may have to do this a number of times to release those ribs. This exercise will help you release, rather than hold onto, the lower back.

When you are singing, as you inhale for each new phrase make sure that you breathe into your hands. This emphasis on the lower back ribs will give you a nice balance of abdominal and back rib expansion for the breath, and prevent an unsightly abdomen and a collapsed chest.

For a Feeling of a "Deep" Breath

1. With your feet wide apart, squat down (hold onto something very stable like both handles on either side of a door if you need support and keep your head straight), and allow yourself to feel your breathing deep in your pelvic floor. This is an area that many people hold tightly; for a good in-breath, it needs to be released. Sing or speak in this position. You will find that you get a wonderful connection with your whole body. The sound will have much more resonance and depth.

2. While sitting in a chair, feel yourself expanding all the way to the bottom of the chair on inhalation. You can do this while watching TV or at your desk at work. In doing this, you will release the abdominal muscles and allow a deeper movement of the diaphragm. Also, you will gain the benefit of added calm.

ACCESSORY MUSCLES

Accessory muscles are generally considered to be those that can aid in an action when the primary muscles for that action are disabled or not able to function fully. For example, the chest muscle, the pectoralis major, normally functions to rotate the arm inward. The origin of the muscle is on the chest, which is very stable, and the insertion is in the upper arm, which is highly mobile. However, if you are doing something like climbing a tree, the arm must remain very stable and then the pectoral muscle can bring the chest to the arm. This is not a movement you need in vocal performance. Many vocal and medical anatomy books contain long lists of accessory muscles (the pectoralis major and minor are examples). If you are using these muscles for making sound, you are using far too many muscles. For best voice use, accessory muscles are not considered important to activate. Rather, they contract to help stabilize the body so that it functions efficiently.

In some anatomy texts you will find long discussions about the sets of intercostal muscles that run between each rib. Current thinking recognizes these muscles as having a stabilizing role for the rib cage rather than as actively participating in the separate actions of inspiration and expiration.

Neck muscles such as the scalenes and the sternocleidomastoids that run from the cervical vertebrae and the skull also stabilize the rib cage during inspiration. Because the larynx has to remain flexible and responsive during performance, it is important that the neck muscles play a stabilizing, rather than an overly active or interfering, role in inspiration.

EXHALATION

During active expiration all the elements of passive breathing are present. However, the key factor here is the additional support given by the abdominal muscles. A girdle of three large muscles covers the abdomen (see figure 3.5). These muscles, the external and internal abdominal obliques and transversus abdominus, function reflexively when physical alignment is good. They contract as a unit to put pressure on the contents of the abdomen, which in turn encourages the upward return of the diaphragm. Abdominal muscle contraction aids the balance of pressures for maintaining efficient breath use. It helps to think of the muscles contracting low in the abdomen and aiming in the direction of the lower back ribs.

A paired, vertical, long muscle, called the rectus abdominus, runs from the lower ribs in front to the pubic bone. It is less

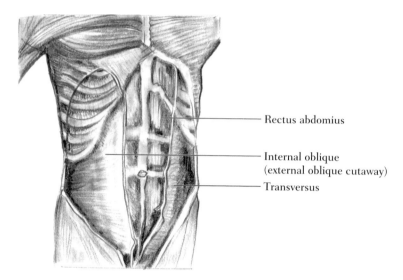

FIGURE 3.5
Muscles of the abdomen

active in the use of the voice, but is thought to add to a little extra top-up breath where text or music need more emphasis.

Many physical fitness routines, such as Pilates, Yoga exercises, and sport techniques, teach people to exhale with movement. This keeps the energy moving and maintains a dynamic adjustment of the muscles as they exercise. The same is true for dramatic voice use. In fact, consider exhaling first and allowing the inhalation to become a reflex action. Below are some suggestions and exercises to encourage efficient exhalation.

Developing Efficient Exhalation

The exercises below are meant to give you a feeling for efficient exhalation and to help you develop the habits that will serve you well in performance. Many performers go into panic mode when faced with an audience. This causes the respiratory pattern to move high in the chest and the abdomen to be forgotten. The breathing support for the voice becomes nonexistent.

1. Stretch your arms up as high as possible, and use a *pssh* or hissing sound between the teeth to blow out until you are out of breath. Do not allow your arms or body to collapse, but maintain your stretch the whole time. This exercise puts your shoulders and chest out of action, because of the stretch, and causes the abdominal muscles to have to work. This is a way of getting those muscles to recognize the need to function. Once you have exhaled, maintain the stretch to allow the air to reenter your lungs as a reflex.

2. As you sing or recite a phrase, move your arms up slowly for the entire length of the phrase.

3. If you are stuck or cannot seem to get a feeling of excitement or energy into the sound, sit in a chair and sing while stamping your feet on the floor as fast as possible. You will be amazed at the sound that comes out. It is common for the feet to hesitate or stop when there is any doubt in the mind of the performer. Do not allow the stomping to stop. You will find that, by moving, the breath will continue to flow, and the voice and body will respond very differently. This exercise prevents the body from going into a holding pattern and allows the sound to be released. It is only an indication that being dynamic inside is a necessary part of singing. The trick is to allow that dynamism to continue when you then stand to sing and are not moving your feet.

THE BALANCE OF THE RESPIRATORY MECHANISM IN SINGING

All the above is stated from an ideal perspective and based on good, dynamic posture. However, rarely does the inexperienced, and only sometimes the experienced, performer have all respiratory factors functioning perfectly. Physical compensation usually occurs somewhere in the body, and each compensatory movement is likely to impair the efficient functioning of the vocal mechanism. Any tension or distortion in the rib cage, especially the back, will prevent adequate intake of air; tension and/or distortion in the neck will cause pressure on the larynx and pharynx and prevent efficient phonation and regulation of air.

The body maintains a delicate balance between the abdomen, chest, and neck to allow optimal use of breath in singing. Ideally, the muscles of the air passages, pharynx, chest, and abdomen are responsive rather than tense. The air pressure is regulated by the muscles at the base of the pelvis (the pelvic floor), the diaphragm, the movement of the rib cage, and the expiratory air pressure on the vocal folds from below (subglottic pressure). The back pressure when the air hits palate and teeth to reflect back toward the vocal folds from above also affects air pressure (see figure 3.6).

Ideally, all of the above is initiated by the intention to sing followed by the appropriate response of the body, rather than by forcing the act of breathing in a conscious and inhibited way. Once the act of breathing grows overly conscious, it becomes less efficient and overbreathing becomes likely. Overbreathing causes the performer to take too much air and lock the chest at the end of the breath. It is then very difficult to begin the sound easily, and spontaneity of performance is unlikely in this circumstance. Persons with poor breathing patterns will have to practice new habits in a conscious manner to create new subconscious, spontaneous reflexes.

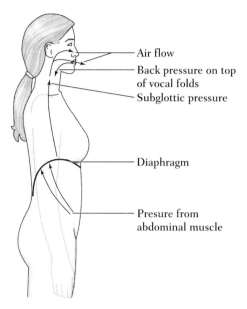

FIGURE 3.6
Balance of pressures in phonation

A singer, or any performer, with efficient breathing is free of obvious physical distortions such as tension around the mouth, protrusion of the jaw, fixation in the face, tightness around the neck, rigidity of the chest, and an unsightly, bulging abdomen. The breath is silent rather than gasping or gulped, and full movement of the diaphragm and movement in the back portion of the lower ribs are possible.

COMMON PROBLEMS THAT PREVENT EFFICIENT BREATHING

Some inefficient breathing patterns can be seen regularly with inexperienced and experienced vocal artists. They may be caused by a variety of problems, including poor physical alignment, too little or too much body tension, or confusion about the breathing process itself. Once these habits become ingrained, they are difficult to change. Common breathing problems include the following:

Raising the shoulders to inhale and pushing them down to exhale. This usually occurs because there is no movement in the lower back and abdomen. Singers and dancers who hold in their tummies excessively are prone to breathe this way. Furthermore, many performers push down the area around the clavicle at the beginning of each phrase. Although sometimes incredibly subtle, it is happening nevertheless and interferes with efficient breath control. To counteract this, it helps to think of having an upper chest that is wide from front to back and that provides a large space for the neck and head to sit on the shoulders.

Holding the back rigid. This limits the excursion of the diaphragm in the area where it has the greatest capability of movement, the back, and causes distortion of the abdomen—usually in the shape of a large bulge. This may occur because the performer thinks he or she is supposed to have great forward excursion in the belly. Allowing the abdomen to bulge tends to pull the spine forward and out of place. This excessive bulge makes it difficult to regulate the expiratory airflow, and the singer then loses the natural elastic physical position for optimal breath use.

Misunderstanding about breathing on the part of the performer. There are so many pet theories regarding the breathing process that it is very likely that many performers are confused about their breathing. Always look to the logic of the body first.

General slackness in the body. This is a result of a lack of stretch and alignment of the body. It leads to poor muscle response generally and a breathy tone.

Generalized tension in the body. Such overall physical tension leads to constriction of the airways and inhibits air intake. It can result in an unpleasant, tense tone quality.

Gasping for breath at the ends of phrases. Many performers are overly conscious of the need for breath, and as a result they end each phrase with a gasp for air while in a panic about getting air for the next phrase. This habit is extremely detrimental to good voice use, and it upsets the onset of an efficient vocal sound.

Awareness of common breathing problems can help you monitor and improve your own breathing. Work with a mirror, a partner, or a teacher to identify such problems. Many are easy to correct if you are aware of them.

Exercise for a Feeling of Ease of Continuity of Breath and Sound

Do this very calming exercise while sitting with both feet on the floor and back lengthened. You will need to work at it in order to get it. This exercise is useful for onset of vocal sound as well. Learning new repertoire this way can alleviate breath problems such as overbreathing or gasping. You want to learn to have a continuity of air in and sound out with no hesitation or gasps along the way.

1. Simply remain calm and notice your breath.
2. Note where in the cycle of air-in-and-air-out the breath changes from inhalation to exhalation.
3. As the breath changes from inhalation to exhalation, mark this point by making a short *hmm* sound.
4. Now comes the tricky part. Allow your hand to follow this breathing pattern by creating a circle *in front* of you with a very specific direction (as if you have a ball on your stomach). As you breathe in, move your hand (and arm) away from the front of your body, with the lowest part of the circle beginning at the level of your pelvis and

the highest at the level of the collarbone. Your hand will be at the highest point of the circle when the breath changes from inhalation to exhalation. As you exhale, the hand will continue the circle toward your body (see figure 3.7).

By moving the hand away from the front of the body in an upward arc as you inhale, you are given a feeling of expanding. Then, as the hand returns downward and in toward the body, there is a feeling of lengthening and getting taller to exhale.

5. Continue using your hand to mimic the physical breath cycle while making the *hmm* sound at the top of the circle. As you continue the exercise, allow the *hmm* to sound longer.

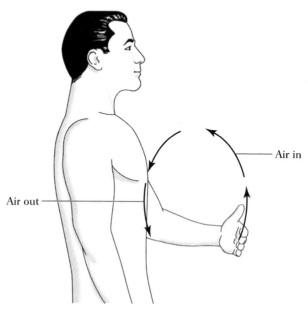

FIGURE 3.7
Direction of the hand for breathing exercise

6. From here on the rule will be the following: As long as you are making sound, the hand will be moving down and away from your body (see figure 3.8).

7. Now, while continuing the circle with your hand, add words such as "hello, how are you" or a phrase of a simple song like a nursery rhyme instead of the *hmm* sound. The words begin at the moment of exhalation.

8. Finally, sing a whole song or speak a passage of text using this method.

The rule is: Air in, sound out. There are no hitches or breaks. As long as your hand is moving in the circle, the air calmly continues. And as long as you are speaking or singing, the

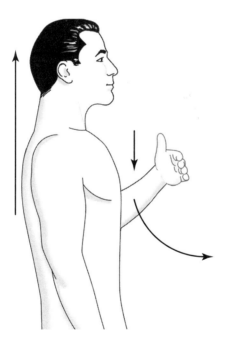

FIGURE 3.8
Movement of hand for exhalation
Feel yourself growing taller as the hand moves down

hand moves. The cycle never stops. Even a momentary hesitation with your mind will tend to make the hand slow down or stop. Have a partner monitor this for you.

BREATHING IS PART OF A BALANCED VOCAL TECHNIQUE

Performers and their teachers spend a great deal of time working with the breath. Although this is critical to effective and efficient voice production, it can be overemphasized to the point of inhibiting the performer and causing him or her to become tense and afraid of the act of breathing—something we do easily most of the time. In context, breathing for performance is simply part of the whole package. It needs to be looked at only when a problem arises.

One day efficient, easy breathing will be emphasized in early education, and teachers in the performing arts will be relieved of the task of correcting patterns that have been neglected or ill gained. Teachers will then feel they can concentrate on other important aspects of voice production.

Easy breathing and silky, seamless sound are the goals of most performers. Any artist will tell you that when it is easy to breathe, the sound *seems* to come with little or no effort. This makes the attention to the breath worthwhile.

4

Making Sound

The vibration that creates voiced sound emanates from two muscular shelves called the vocal folds (also called vocal cords). They are located in the larynx, which is suspended in the neck by muscles from above and below. Basically, the larynx is the house for a buzzer (sound), which is activated by airflow from the lungs and modified and amplified by the resonator (the pharynx). The lengthening and shortening of the vocal folds determines pitch. If you have ever blown up a balloon, pulled the opening wide to release air, and listened to the resulting squeal, you will have a good idea of how the vocal folds work. By analogy, the more stretched the mouth of your balloon, the higher its squeal.

The vocal folds are the most researched area of the vocal mechanism, and as a result there is more scientific literature on vocal fold function than on any other aspect of vocal production. Also, it is the vocal folds' appearance and movement that doctors use to make an initial diagnosis when they examine your voice. In the field of voice, there is thus a great deal of emphasis on the vocal folds. While this is important scientifically and medically, it is just one element of the picture. Bear in mind, as you study, that the larynx, which houses the vocal folds, is only part of the whole. The larynx is part of the vocal tract, which includes the pharynx, part of the respiratory system, and it is also related to the digestive system by way of the pharynx. Taken out of context, the information can be misleading.

The larynx evolved as part of the respiratory system and is considered the protector of the lungs. The cartilages that form the larynx sit on top of the trachea, and the vocal folds close tightly when you swallow to keep food or foreign material from entering your lungs. The vocal folds are so sensitive that you will cough if you inhale anything larger than three microns (smaller than a particle of dust) in diameter. This is why minute airborne toxins are so harmful to the lungs.

The larynx thus has two main functions: it acts, first, as a valve to protect the lungs and, second, as a mechanism for producing sound. When we swallow, the throat constricts to send the food downward. The pharynx narrows, the larynx rises, and the vocal folds close tightly, thereby causing the food to go down the esophagus rather than into your lungs. Singing in the "swallowing position," that is, with the pharynx partially constricted, will not give you a very pleasing voice quality. This point is discussed in chapter 5. Effective singing and speaking demand the opposite—a wide-open air passageway (the throat) with no constriction or hindrance to the balance of the larynx in the neck or its ability to vibrate freely. To understand this better, we need to explore more details of the larynx.

AN OVERVIEW OF THE ANATOMY OF THE LARYNX

The larynx is suspended and supported in the neck from in front, behind, above, and below by groups of paired muscles (see figure 4.1). Therefore, the complexity of the laryngeal relationship with

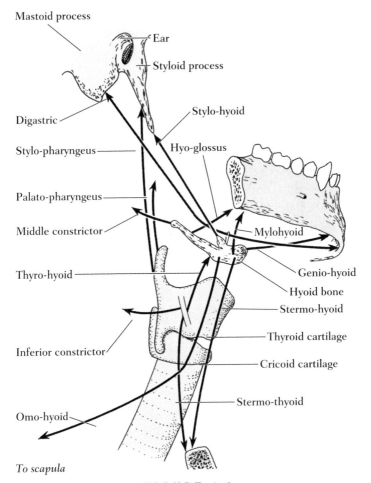

FIGURE 4.1

Diagram of muscles suspending the larynx in neck

The complexities and interrelationships of the muscles of the head and neck make it difficult to assess readily definitive muscle action in speech and singing. However, it can be clearly shown here that changes in position of the larynx, pharynx, and tongue inevitably affect the shape of the vocal tract.

the rest of your neck, throat (the pharynx, soft palate, tongue, jaw), and chest must not be underestimated. Even though the larynx can be seen as a separate unit, it never functions in that manner. The position of the neck and chest, movement and tension of the tongue and jaw, and flexibility or constriction of the muscles of the pharynx all contribute to laryngeal efficiency and affect tone quality. This is why it is dangerous to make too many assumptions about its specific actions at any given time.

THE SKELETAL FRAMEWORK OF THE LARYNX

The skeleton of the larynx consists of four cartilages—the cricoid, the thyroid, and two arytenoids (see figure 4.2). The hyoid bone is sometimes included in the structure because of its muscular connection to the thyroid cartilage.

The skeletal framework consists of the following:

- The cricoid cartilage, the base of the larynx, sits on top of the trachea. It forms a complete circle and is shaped like a signet or class ring, with the large portion at the back (like a class ring worn backward).
- Two tiny pyramid-shaped cartilages, the arytenoids, sit on top of the back of the cricoid. They have a joint structure that allows them to tilt on the cricoid as well as slide from side to side. The muscular process at the sides of these cartilages is where several of the muscles that move the vocal folds attach. The vocal process at the front is one attachment of the vocal fold.

Remember that a process is something that sticks out. And yet there is no real reason that the horns of the thyroid cartilage are not called processes. They just aren't. Sorry. You will just have to remember that.

- The thyroid cartilage, or Adam's apple, is shaped somewhat like a shield and is closed in front and open in back. It has two projections, or horns—a superior horn, where a number

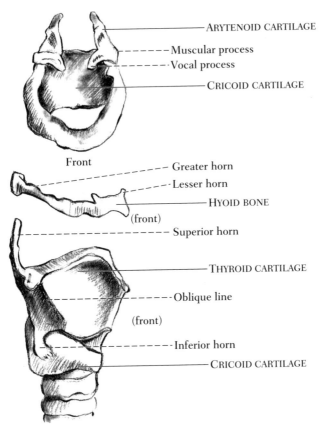

ARYTENOID CARTILAGE

Muscular process

Vocal process

CRICOID CARTILAGE

Front

Greater horn

Lesser horn

HYOID BONE

(front)

Superior horn

THYROID CARTILAGE

Oblique line

(front)

Inferior horn

CRICOID CARTILAGE

FIGURE 4.2
Skeletal framework of larynx

of muscles from the palate and pharynx attach, and an inferior horn, which forms a joint with the cricoid cartilage. This joint allows the thyroid or cricoid cartilage to tilt slightly.

- The hyoid bone is a horseshoe-shaped bone suspended just below the mandible, and is usually included in any discussion of the larynx. It shares muscles with the pharynx, mandible, and larynx.
- A small elastic cartilage called the epiglottis is not really considered an active part of the vocal mechanism. It covers the

vocal folds when you swallow and helps keep food out. However, people who have had it removed have had few problems keeping food out of the lungs, because the vocal folds close so tightly when one swallows.

The best way to understand these cartilages is to make a model of the larynx. Artistry is not important here; it is the process of working with the material and looking at the detail of the larynx that is valuable.

Making a Model Larynx

One of the best ways to understand the larynx is to make a three-dimensional clay (plasticine seems to work best) model of the cartilages. By following the guidelines below for building a larynx, you will acquire a thorough grasp of its structure and a basis for understanding how the muscles work.

1. Begin by building the cricoid cartilage as a base. Look carefully at its shape before you start. The front is deceptively narrow, and the back is higher and steeper than you think. Some people like to build a solid trachea for it to sit on, but this is not necessary, since the bottom of the cricoid is almost level.

2. Now look very carefully at the shape of the arytenoid cartilages, and create them. Note their relative proportion to the cricoid and thyroid. It is worth measuring your picture or diagram to determine the ratio. Now sit them on the back of the cricoid cartilage. Find a good illustration, and look carefully at the shape of the arytenoid and cricoid joint articulations.

3. Next build the thyroid cartilage. Again look carefully at its features and dimensions. Many people do not allow

for the depth of the thyroid or for how far back on the cricoid the facet for the joint is located.

4. You may wish to add the vocal folds that attach to the vocal process of the arytenoids and the inside front of the thyroid.

5. If you wish, you can now attach the epiglottis to the inside front of the thyroid cartilage just above the attachment of the vocal folds. The indentations you see on the epiglottis are places where mucous glands sit. They help keep the larynx moist.

6. You can now make the hyoid bone, which is shaped somewhat like a horseshoe. Notice that it has lesser and greater horns. You will probably need some toothpicks to hold it in place and suspend it above the thyroid cartilage.

Now that you have a structure with which to work, you can learn more about the muscles of the larynx. Take some cloth material, like a ribbon, and cut it in the shape of the muscles and stick it on with pins.

THE INTRINSIC MUSCLES OF THE LARYNX

Vocal fold movements are created by several sets of paired muscles (see figure 4.3). First to breathe, the vocal folds must move apart. The posterior crico-arytenoid muscles cause this to happen. For efficient phonation, the vocal folds must come together very cleanly and evenly. This is accomplished by two sets of muscles, the lateral crico-arytenoids and the inter-arytenoids. To elongate the folds for pitch changes, the crico-thyroid muscles contract. The muscle of the vocal fold is called the vocalis, and its contraction can cause the folds to thicken and slightly move apart (see figure 4.4). To understand the actions of these muscles, we must learn the detail of each cartilage. Some of the most important muscles and their functions are listed below.

Any discussion of muscle action is based on what the muscle would do if it could act on its own, without antagonism from any other source. In some ways this is an abnormal situation, because we humans like to interfere with nature and create muscular antagonism when it is not needed. For the purposes of learning, however, you have to start from what is possible.

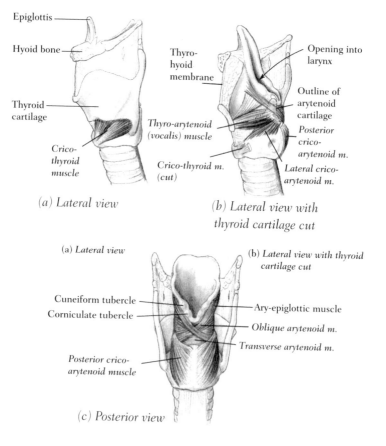

Epiglottis

Hyoid bone

Thyroid cartilage

Crico-thyroid muscle

Thyro-hyoid membrane

Thyro-arytenoid (vocalis) muscle

Crico-thyroid m. (cut)

Opening into larynx

Outline of arytenoid cartilage

Posterior crico-arytenoid m.

Lateral crico-arytenoid m.

(a) Lateral view

(b) Lateral view with thyroid cartilage cut

(a) Lateral view

(b) Lateral view with thyroid cartilage cut

Cuneiform tubercle
Corniculate tubercle

Posterior crico-arytenoid muscle

Ary-epiglottic muscle

Oblique arytenoid m.

Transverse arytenoid m.

(c) Posterior view

FIGURE 4.3
Muscles of the larynx

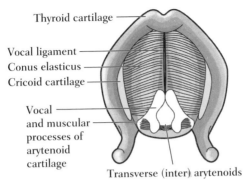

Thyroid cartilage

Vocal ligament
Conus elasticus
Cricoid cartilage

Vocal
and muscular
processes of
arytenoid
cartilage

Transverse (inter) arytenoids

F I G U R E   4 . 4
Partial closure of vocal folds

The paired posterior crico-arytenoid muscles are located at the back of the cricoid cartilage and attach to the lateral portion (muscular process) of each arytenoid cartilage. Their contraction causes the vocal processes of the arytenoids to swing away from the midline, thus opening the space between the vocal folds (the glottis) and creating a space for air to enter the lungs. This happens subconsciously.

To make a clear sound, the vocal folds must come together evenly in the midline. Two sets of muscles are needed for this: the lateral crico-arytenoids, which swing the vocal processes toward each other, and the inter-arytenoids, which slide the two arytenoid cartilages toward the middle. When the inter-arytenoid muscles do not contract adequately, the resultant tone is breathy because air is escaping at a chink left between the vocal processes of the arytenoid cartilages.

The crico-thyroid muscles attach to the front of the cricoid cartilage and the front lateral edge (inside and outside) of the thyroid cartilage (see figure 4.5). When these muscles contract, the thyroid and cricoid cartilages are tilted away from each other; the thyroid moves forward and the cricoid backward. This action causes the vocal folds to stretch and the pitch to go higher. You can test this by singing a note and shortening the folds by very

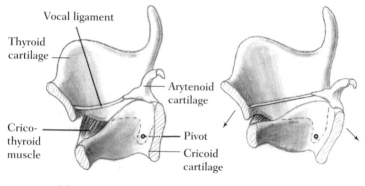

(a) Inactive muscles,
slack vocal ligaments

(b) Contraction of
muscles, tilting of thyroid
and cricoid cartilages

FIGURE 4.5
Action of crico-thyroid muscles

gently pushing on the front of the thyroid cartilage. The pitch
will go down involuntarily.

The muscular portion of the vocal folds is made up of the
thyro-arytenoid muscles. The vocal folds consist of three parts:
the internal thyro-arytenoid (known as the vocalis muscles), the
vocal ligament (the shiny white part of the vocal folds seen in
pictures and professional videos), and the vocal processes of the
arytenoid cartilages (see figure 4.6).

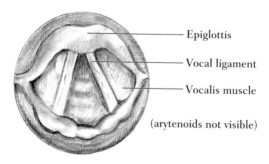

FIGURE 4.6
The vocal folds

The muscles of the vocal folds have the potential to draw the thyroid and arytenoid cartilages closer together. However, the posterior crico-arytenoid and crico-thyroid muscles can oppose this action. It is thought that contraction of the vocalis causes the vocal folds to become thicker and create a heavier sound. Excess tension in these muscles is considered responsible for uneven changes of voice called register breaks.

PITCH AND REGISTER

The vocal folds vibrate at the same number of cycles per second as the pitch they create. For example, to create A 440, the folds vibrate 440 times per second. The vocal folds vibrate with differing degrees of thickness, according to the pitch and amount of elongation involved. A tone that has low frequencies and pitch is produced by thick vocal folds that meet very firmly at the midline at each vibration. High pitches and frequencies are produced by vocal folds that have thin edges as a result of being elongated. For effective singing, the change of vocal fold length and thickness from low pitches to high ones must be smooth and graduated. When antagonistic muscles do not release as the pitch ascends, the vocal folds are prevented from stretching properly, the tone becomes heavy and forced, and breaks in register can occur.

THE ONSET OF SOUND

The coordination of breath and vocal fold closure is important for the onset of tone, sometimes called the attack. When closure is inadequate, the tone is breathy. This can occur for a number of reasons: poor vocal coordination, weak inter-arytenoid muscles, swelling because of allergies, overuse, abuse, vocal nodules, and other pathology that alters the smooth edges of the vocal folds.

When the vocal folds are closed too tightly, the onset of tone becomes harsh and explosive. This explosion occurs because pressurized air below the vocal folds bursts out. This so-called glottal attack can over time contribute to vocal abuse and cause problems such as nodules and vocal fatigue.

The ideal sound made by the vocal folds is clean and clear. However, when the coordination of posture, breath, and onset of the tone is not balanced, the sound can be less than ideal. Below are some ways to explore the various sounds you can make. And sometimes you do want a breathy quality or a deliberately ugly sound. It depends entirely on the context. But you do not want an unhealthy sound.

Characteristics of Vocal Sound

Choose several phrases of a song or text. Then sing or speak with a partner, and listen to what happens to the other person's voice when you experiment with the habits below. You can't really experiment if you are trying to listen to your voice and do the task.

1. What happens to the tone when you perform your phrases in the following ways:
   - with poor posture
   - with so much abdominal pressure that the vocal folds are thrust apart at the onset of sound
   - by means of poor breathing patterns such as pulling the chest down
   - by deliberately producing a breathy sound
   - by holding the breath before beginning the tone

These will usually produce a breathy voice quality. If you know what causes it, you can begin to find a way to change.

2. Using the same song or text, listen to what happens to the tone when you perform them in the following ways:
   • with postural tension
   • by pushing the head forward or throwing it back to begin to sing or speak
   • by pushing the jaw forward or pulling it down to pronounce consonants or vowels
   • by pulling the back of the tongue down
   • with too much pressure in the chest, which in turn produces excess subglottic pressure

The above tasks will usually produce an overly tense sound. Many performers, however, display these very common habits.

VIBRATO

It is natural for the voice to have some vibrato. Pop singers tend to be frightened of hearing this in their heads. It makes them think they will sound like an opera singer. However, it takes more than vibrato to make a singer sound *classical*. The danger for performers is trying to make the tone too straight. This can put a lot of pressure on the vocal mechanism and create vocal problems.

Most easily produced, free vocal sounds have a vibrato of between five and eight pulsations per second. A vibrato of less than five pulsations per second will be heard as separate pitches and sound like a wobble. A tone with more than eight per second will sound more like a bleat or tremolo. This excessive vibrato is caused by too much pressure on the vocal folds and is unpleasant to the ear.

Vibrato creates an illusion of true pitch. It can deviate as much as a half step or semitone around the pitch and still be perceived by the listener as tolerable. A good vibrato has a regular rate and interval and is consistent around the pitch. You can see your vibrato if you visit an acoustics lab or download one of the free speech analysis packages from the internet. If you have a chance to do this, you can experiment with what happens with normal, excessive, or little vibrato.

Exercises for Coordination of the Vocal Folds

The coordination of the vocal folds and the onset of vocal sound is one key to vocal efficiency. When the coordination is inefficient, it can cause problems with the breathing mechanism and make a performer substitute some unwanted action in the neck and shoulders. All of these can affect the rate of vibrato as well.

The exercises below are intended to help you create an efficient beginning to your voiced sound.

1. Use a tiny childlike half cry or whimper to get the sensation of a clean onset of sound.
2. On an *ng*, gently siren your voice from high to low. Make sure the lips and jaw are relaxed when you do this. When you are comfortable with the *ng*, experiment with other vowels.
3. Use a gentle laugh on the syllable *hee* throughout your vocal range.
4. Sing phrases or songs on the vowel *ee*. The *ee* vowel tends to help a breathy sound because it brings about complete closure of the vocal folds.
5. Imagine you are speaking or singing with the widest possible neck and upper chest. Having a wide upper chest has nothing to do with raising your chest.

6. Gently turn your head from side to side as if you are say-ing "no" before and after you take your breath and begin your sound. This will prevent you from holding on to the breath or the neck as you begin to phonate.

COORDINATION

Phonation basically occurs at subconscious levels. However, per-formers will go through quite a checklist to begin a sound effi-ciently and clearly. They must conceive the pitch and the quality of tone and emotion desired, take a breath with no interfering tension, and begin the tone with clarity and precision. Profes-sionals seem to achieve this easily, whereas the inexperienced vocal artist struggles. When you have good coordination of your alignment, efficient breath flow, and freedom of the neck, jaw, and tongue, the onset of sound will be no problem. It is usually the momentary panic of beginnings and the holding of the breath that create the most problems.

Efficient phonation is not always easy to learn and has to be done largely by trial and error. At this point a good teacher can be very helpful. When the coordination becomes consistent and habitual, the act of phonation can be relegated to the subcon-scious and attention paid to the performance instead.

5

The Structures of Resonance
and Voice Quality

Aesthetically, the most important aspect of the voice is resonance, which comes mainly from the pharynx, a part of the vocal tract. The quality of the human voice is unique with every individual; and at the same time it is the most difficult to study and quantify. Verbal descriptions of tone can only vaguely convey what is a kinesthetic (or sensed) understanding. This is a minefield for those in the vocal arts because everyone perceives sensation differently. Therefore, the adjustments that alter quality involve very much trial and error for performers, and they pose a challenge to find an adequate language for those working with them.

Understanding the pharynx and vocal tract entails knowing the anatomical interrelationships of the muscles of the soft palate, pharynx, tongue, lips, jaw, hyoid bone, and larynx. Because of the physical complexity of these relationships, the majority of the current research in this area focuses on building computer models of the vocal tract and studying the acoustics. If you look on the internet, you will find many websites that feature vocal tract modeling and videos of it in action.

The various shapes of the vocal tract determine voice quality. The vocal tract consists of the physical spaces that respond to the vibrations of the vocal folds to create what we know as vocal resonance. These spaces are composed mainly of the mouth and pharynx, which is divided into the nasal, oral, and laryngeal portions (see figure 5.1). The vibrations made by the vocal folds are reflected into the various areas of the pharynx, and are either

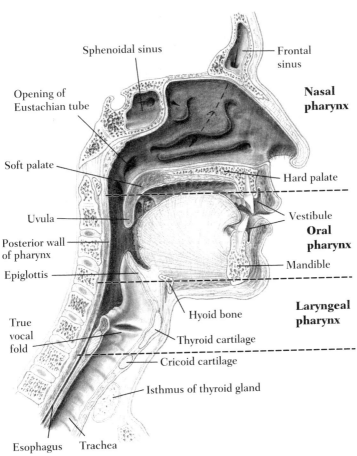

FIGURE 5.1

The vocal tract and divisions of the pharynx

reinforced or inhibited by the shape of the space or by the quality of the walls of the structures and membranes.

The ultimate quality of any sound is the result of the combination of the shape of the pharynx (throat), general vocal and whole-body coordination, and a vivid imagination. Physically, for optimal resonance, a singer or speaker will have a throat that is flexible and able to respond to the performer's intentions, a lifted soft palate, a flexible ready tongue and a jaw that hangs nicely in place. These are the ingredients that allow the mechanism of resonance to respond to the imagination. The possibilities for vocal color are endless.

Anatomically, the pharynx serves as a dual passageway for food and air. It separates into definitive roles only at the larynx and esophagus. In chewing and swallowing, the action is to elevate and narrow the space in order to send food into the esophagus. At that point the vocal folds close tightly to prevent food from entering the lungs. For optimal voice use, this same area has to be spacious and relaxed, and the top of the esophagus closes off to prevent air from entering the stomach.

The anatomy of the larynx was already discussed in chapter 4. Some further discussion is necessary in this chapter because of the larynx's intimate relationship with the pharynx. It is, however, various parts of the pharynx that create most of the resonance and help contribute to the shapes the vowels, vital ingredients of any vocal artist's toolbox. (The subject of vowels and their shapes is discussed in chapter 6.)

AN OVERVIEW OF THE ANATOMY
OF THE PHARYNX

Anatomically, the muscles of the pharynx have been described as a flexible sleeve that hangs from the base of the skull, with openings into the nose, mouth, and larynx. This sleeve is formed by several groups of muscles that attach to bones and cartilages on the skull, the mandible, the hyoid bone, and the larynx.

THE SKELETAL STRUCTURE OF THE PHARYNX

The skeletal structures and ligaments to which the pharyngeal muscles attach include the following (see figure 5.2):

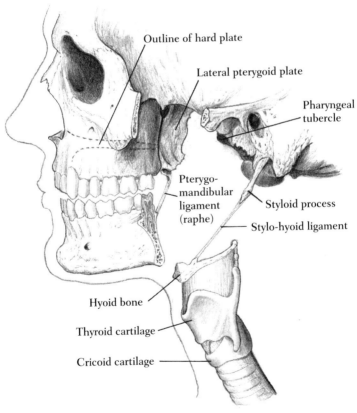

Outline of hard plate

Lateral pterygoid plate

Pharyngeal tubercle

Pterygo-mandibular ligament (raphe)

Styloid process

Stylo-hyoid ligament

Hyoid bone

Thyroid cartilage

Cricoid cartilage

FIGURE 5.2
The skeletal structure of the pharynx

- a small bump (the pharyngeal tubercle) on the base of the occipital bone of the skull
- the styloid process, of the temporal bone
- the styloid ligament, located between the styloid bone and the lesser horn of the hyoid bone
- the pterygoid plates of the sphenoid bone
- the pterygo-mandibular ligament between the medial pterygoid plate and the lingula of the mandible
- the mandible
- the hyoid bone
- the thyroid and the cricoid cartilages

From these bones, cartilages, and ligaments, the muscles of the pharynx form the muscular sleeve with openings into the nose, mouth, and larynx (see figure 5.3). Each of these openings relates to one of the three divisions of the pharynx: the nasal, oral, and laryngeal pharynges, each with its own sound quality. A nasal quality is the result of air escaping through the nose, the oral pharynx is where most of the resonance of the voice occurs, and the opening of the larynx is considered to have a resonance peculiar to trained singers. The muscular sleeve continues as the esophagus.

THE MUSCLES OF THE PHARYNX

The muscles forming the pharynx consist of two layers: an outer layer consisting of three constrictors, whose fibers have a circular direction, and an inner longitudinal group coming down from the skull and palate (see figures 5.3 and 5.4).

The three constrictor muscles are named superior, middle, and inferior; acting as a unit, they combine with the longitudinal muscles to narrow and shorten the throat in order to squeeze food down to the esophagus. Their origins from the skull, hyoid bone, and larynx are complex. Ideally, they would have no major

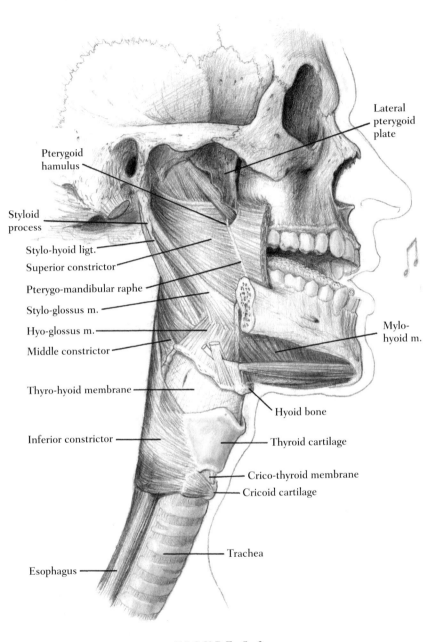

FIGURE 5.3
Pharyngeal constrictors

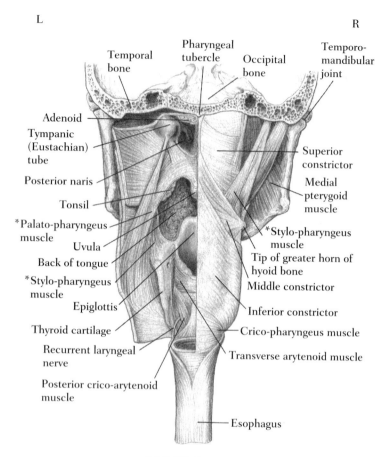

L

R

Temporal bone

Pharyngeal tubercle

Occipital bone

Temporo-mandibular joint

Adenoid

Tympanic (Eustachian) tube

Posterior naris

Tonsil

*Palato-pharyngeus muscle

Uvula

Back of tongue

*Stylo-pharyngeus muscle

Epiglottis

Thyroid cartilage

Recurrent laryngeal nerve

Posterior crico-arytenoid muscle

Superior constrictor

Medial pterygoid muscle

*Stylo-pharyngeus muscle

Tip of greater horn of hyoid bone

Middle constrictor

Inferior constrictor

Crico-pharyngeus muscle

Transverse arytenoid muscle

Esophagus

FIGURE 5.4
Longitudinal muscles of the pharynx
See starred muscles

active role in voice use. Any small changes, however, in their levels of tension, or gradations of release, cause the shape of the throat to change and influence voice quality. Whether a performer can, or would want to, control consciously any or all of the constrictors during performance is unknown. What most singers and speakers desire is space in the throat for resonance. This happens when the pharyngeal muscles are relaxed. Family speech patterns, regional dialect, and one's native language usually determine general patterns and habitual use of the pharyngeal muscles and the soft palate, tongue, and lips.

The layer of longitudinal muscles is responsible for shortening the pharynx in swallowing. These muscles are paired and include the stylo-pharyngeus and the palato-pharyngeus. When they contract, they pull up the larynx and the lower portion of the pharynx.

There are a number of reasons why you might want to know the details of the muscles of the pharynx. First, you will have more information about the unlimited possibilities of what can happen in its complex relationship with the soft palate, tongue, and larynx. Second, it will enable you to observe with more awareness—and question, rather than just accept—any explanation you are given. And last, you will realize that the pharynx functions incredibly well when we get rid of any bad habits associated with breathing and speech patterns.

The details of the muscles have been put in the box below. If you prefer to skip this information, you can thus do it easily.

Muscles of the Pharynx

You will not be able to see all of the attachments of these muscles, because other muscles or structures sometimes overlap them. Careful study of the illustrations in this book and those listed in its "Further Reading" will help you to see these muscles better. Begin by finding all the bony and cartilaginous structures mentioned above (see figures 5.1 and 5.2). Next, get a general overview of the pharynx. Then look at and trace specific muscles you want to understand better.

1. The superior constrictor has multiple *origins* from:
   - the pterygo-mandibular raphe (a raphe is a line formed by muscles coming together from opposing sides)
   - the mandible
   - a small slip of muscle from the tongue
   - the medial pterygoid plate

   It *inserts* into:
   - the pharyngeal tubercle on the occipital bone
   - the posterior midline pharyngeal raphe at the back

2. The middle constrictor *originates* from:
   - the greater horn of the hyoid bone
   - the lower third of stylo-hyoid ligament

   It *inserts* at the back into the pharyngeal raphe.

3. The inferior constrictor has two portions:

   a. The upper part *originates* from:
      - the oblique line of the thyroid cartilage
      - a small fibrous arch linking the thyroid and cricoid cartilages

   It *inserts* at the back into the pharyngeal raphe.

   b. The lower part is continuous and has no raphe

   It runs from one side of the cricoid cartilage to the other. It is given a separate name: the crico-pharyngeus. It is this muscle that contracts to keep air out of the stomach.

4. There are two main longitudinal muscles:

   a. The paired stylo-pharyngeus *originates* from the styloid process on the temporal bone and *inserts* onto the back of the wings of the thyroid cartilage and into the pharyngeal fascia (tissue) behind. Its action causes the raising and tilting of the larynx and the shortening of the pharynx.

   b. The paired palato-pharyngeus *originates* from a portion of the hard and soft palates and also *inserts* on the wings of the thyroid and the pharyngeal fascia. This muscle can also elevate the larynx and base of the pharynx.

THE SOFT PALATE

The soft palate must also be included in any discussion of the pharynx. For efficient speech and singing as well as during swallowing, the soft palate must be raised to prevent extra air from escaping through (and creating unwanted nasal sound) or, in the case of eating, food entering the nose.

The soft palate is made up of a conglomeration of four paired muscles: two above, the levator and tensor palati, and two below, the palato-pharyngeus and the palato-glossus (see figure 5.5). This is an anatomical area where muscular antagonism can create unwanted sound. If the lower connections of the palate are tense—for example the tongue—it is nearly impossible for the palate to achieve enough elevation. This can create problems such as too much nasality and a garbled sound. Chapter 6 discusses this further.

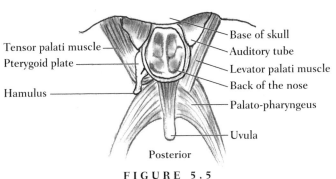

Tensor palati muscle
Pterygoid plate
Hamulus
Base of skull
Auditory tube
Levator palati muscle
Back of the nose
Palato-pharyngeus
Uvula
Posterior

FIGURE 5.5
Muscles of the soft palate

The main muscles that raise the palate are the levator palati, which originate from the pterygoid portion of the sphenoid bone. There is also a set of muscles, the tensor palati, which stretch the palate laterally. They originate from the sphenoid bone and part of the tympanic tube. Their primary action is to help restore the balance of air pressure to the inner ear. This is why sucking or yawning seems to help balance the air pressure in the ears during airplane flights.

The palato-pharyngeus muscle was included in the discussion of the pharynx, and the palato-glossus will be covered in more detail in the description of the tongue in chapter 6.

TENSIONS THAT AFFECT VOCAL QUALITY

By looking closely at figure 5.1 again, you will easily see that any undue tension in the constrictors and longitudinal muscles of the pharynx will pull on a variety of structures in the mouth, throat, and larynx. The variety of shape and movement in the vocal tract is endless. As was stated before, any changes in the shape of the vocal tract and pharynx change the resonance and alter voice quality.

Performers can be seen using excessive effort when learning or when perceiving that they are not working hard enough. They can develop a number of poor habits that affect voice quality. These include the following: overly active facial muscles, especially the mouth and lips, staring, unseeing eyes, the position and action of the mandible, rigidity of the tongue, muscles in the neck that can be seen standing out, chest constriction, and emotional overinvolvement.

You may ask how all of the areas above affect the pharynx. When all of them function efficiently, it is simple. For the majority of performers, however, little inefficient habits can have a domino effect on all the structures in the head and neck. With careful observation you can see and hear many of these.

Exercises for Understanding the Role of Facial Habits in Vocal Resonance

Television gives us ample opportunity to observe well-known performers close-up. The camera makes it easy to spot common poor habits, patterns, and personal character-istics. These are generally the habits that young performers tend to imitate—to their detriment. By observing and ex-ploring what happens with both physical distortion and "normality," you can notice the changes in voice quality they create. The patterns below will give you a good idea of how positive and negative habits contribute to vocal quality.

These exercises are best done in pairs or with a video camera, so that you can have feedback on the vocal quality. When you do this, ask yourself how each of these sounds looks, and whether you would like to watch and listen to a performer who does this.

Choose several phrases of a song or speech and observe what happens when you perform them the following ways:
1. distort the lips with an exaggerated pucker like a kiss
   - pull them inward
   - pull them to one side
   - look natural as if speaking with a friend
2. open the jaw to one side
   - allow it to open naturally
   - hold it open in a fixed way

3. sing or speak with glaring eyes, as if angry with someone
    • with wrinkled brows or a worried look
    • with eyes that look alert and aware and see the audience
4. deliberately pull the tongue down
    • tense or hold on to the inside of your mouth
5. let your face be deadpan with no activity in the muscles of the cheeks
6. have an alive and vibrant face that reflects the meaning of the words

MISCONCEPTIONS ABOUT RESONANCE

As was noted earlier, the complexity of the pharyngeal configuration makes it difficult to research physically. Although X-ray analyses, acoustic studies, and computer tract simulations have focused on the topic, there remain many unanswered questions regarding resonance and voice quality. A number of pedagogy books show drawings of where the tone is felt. However, this is a dangerous practice. How it feels and what is actually happening physically may be quite different. This is easy to understand if you have had the experience of having your posture adjusted, felt you looked strange and awkward, only to see in the mirror or video that you were perfectly fine. The same thing happens with your sense of tone.

Drawings of where the tone is felt can encourage performers to try to place their sound in those places. This leads to misconceptions about where sound is focused and causes constriction, sound limited in both volume and quality, and muscular patterns that are difficult to alter later. Having optimal space, stretch, and body balance will create a focused clear tone without the need to point and aim. Part III has many exercises designed to help you achieve this.

There are many old wives' tales about resonance. When these are investigated from an anatomical point of view, they do not make good sense. Three of the most common misconceptions involve the terms "head resonance," "chest resonance," and "sinus tone." A resonance chamber has to be hollow in order to function properly. As we noted earlier, resonance is the amplification or reinforcement of vibration, normally by a hollow cavity or space. The head and the chest are not hollow but filled with soft material. Such materials have few, if any, resonance properties. Head resonance and chest resonance (or voice) relate to acoustic properties of vocal qualities much like the hi-fi terms "tweeters" and "woofers" or as the highs and lows on a graphic equalizer relate to acoustic properties of recorded sounds. A complete, balanced tone will have elements of both qualities in it, and an accomplished performer will feel this. Balance of vocal quality comes from a whole-body connection and coordination with the sound. The vocal tract can help or hinder this balance, depending on the ease of the performer's technique and the choice of color for character and drama.

Resonators need an opening that allows the resonance to emerge. The sinuses are air-filled cavities, but they have very tiny openings into the nasal cavity the size of a pencil lead. Research on the role of the sinuses in singing shows that there is no perceptible difference in the tone to an audience but that the performer feels the vibration in the face by way of bone conduction.

Singers and speakers are used to feeling the vibration of the bones in the skull, particularly the hard palate, maxilla, and bones around the front of the face, and associating those sensations with the actual resonance. Their inner reality differs from the outer reality that an audience hears. This is one reason that performers are fooled regarding the quality of their sound, and that they often perceive recordings of themselves to be "not like me." When performers become too attached to their inner sound, they find it difficult to be comfortable with positive changes that alter that inner sound, and this can make learning slow, unless there is feedback such as that provided by an excellent teacher, a tape recorder, or a video camera.

Releasing the Vocal Tract

These exercises help you release the muscles of the vocal tract and increase vocal quality. Do them with a partner or video feedback so that you can pay attention to what you are doing and not how you are sounding.

1. Use the sensation of the beginning of a yawn to get the soft palate up and a feeling of space in the throat. It is important not to let the yawn go to a point of excess tension where the tongue begins to tighten.

2. To relax the throat and get the soft palate moving, use an exercise called umming and chewing.

   • With your mouth closed, chew with a lot of lip and tongue movement that would embarrass your mother and, at the same time, make a sustained "umm." It will sound as if you are chewing the "umm."

   • Still with your mouth closed, "umm and chew" a whole song.

   • Next, permit yourself the privilege of allowing an occasional word to slip out.

   • Then "umm and chew" the first section of a phrase, and sing or speak the last part.

   • Finally, sing or speak the words, maintaining the sensations you had while "umming and chewing."

This exercise will begin to break down any habits of holding on to the jaw or tongue as you perform.

3. Make a small circle with your thumb and forefinger as if creating the mouth of a megaphone. Hold it about an inch in front of your mouth, and sing or speak into it. This tends to focus the sound, limit the over opening of the mouth, and help you maintain the space in your vocal tract.

When you open your mouth too wide, the pharynx and soft palate are unable to function normally. There is more about this in chapter 6.

ACHIEVING OPTIMAL QUALITY

When posture, physical balance, good breath and vocal coordination, an alive face and eyes, and an active imagination are present, there is every chance that the vocal tract and pharynx will function efficiently and allow optimal vocal quality in any performer. Where some artists fall short is in believing that the singing and speaking voice do not require the same attention. Bad speech habits can make singing difficult. Moreover, actors with wonderful speaking voices seem to become other persons when asked to sing. The principles of good vocal quality are the same in speech and in singing.

Ideally the best elements of a person's speaking quality are present in the singing voice and vice versa. When singers' singing bears no relation to their speaking, something of their identification and individuality is missing. Optimal vocal quality for each person is present when the voice, body, and imagination are fully integrated.

6

Articulation

Words are what differentiate vocal artists from other performers, such as instrumentalists or mime artists. The need for clarity and clear enunciation of the verbal message is unquestioned. Although the words form only a part of the total communication package of the visible, the voice, and the text, they are essential and cannot be neglected. At the same time, those who overemphasize the words run the risk of neglecting the nonverbal components of communication and having the audience miss the message anyway. Therefore, while you are studying the anatomical structures that enable you to produce the words, bear in mind that words are integral to the total communication.

That said, it is the area of articulation that has so many ingrained habits. We learn to speak at an early age, and the muscular articulation patterns are well developed by the time we begin to think about being a performer. Speech patterns or dialects are derived from parents, friends, and local and national cultural practices, with additional patterns created from physical or psychological balance or imbalance. Each individual develops a set of predominant muscular habits that shape the way vowels and consonants are made. We sometimes call this accent or dialect. When efficient habits of speech are balanced with good physical alignment, the articulation for singing and speaking is much easier. However, that ideal is rarely found in performers today, and teachers spend a great deal of time and attention correcting faulty articulation, which interferes with good vocal production—both the quality of sound and the clarity of text.

The effective performer will look normal without facial distortion. If there is facial distortion such as displacement of the jaw or exaggerated use of the lips, there is likely to be a vocal quality that can be improved. There were exercises relating to this in chapter 5. One of the reasons some classical singers are mimicked is that they can look so amazingly over the top in their efforts to pronounce the text. Singing and dramatic text do not need to look strange. Below are some preliminary observations you can make on yourself and others.

Observing Patterns of Articulation

Many situations can provide you with study material of speech patterns. Begin with yourself and your family. Then begin to observe friends and a variety of performers. Television is a good place to do observation, since newsreaders, talk show hosts, and actors provide some very interesting speech patterns.

You can either use a mirror or video camera to observe yourself or work with a partner and compare notes. Remember that you are just observing for the moment—not making corrections.

1. Look at a performer from the front and side. Notice whether the jaw just hangs or is overactive in some way,

such as excessive opening, opening to one side, protruding to make some consonants and vowels, or clenched. It is most common to see some of these actions when pronouncing the sounds *h*, *ch*, and *j*.

2. Notice how the lips are being used. Are they tense or loose? Do they meet directly in the midline or off to the side? Tense lips tend to have a domino effect inside the vocal tract. Lips that pronounce consonants to the side of the mouth can indicate a speech impediment, particularly when people try to pronounce the *th* sound with the lips rather than with the tongue. Sometimes this pattern also indicates partial deafness on the side to which the lips deviate. These people are speaking or singing to their "good" ear.

3. Is the tongue centered in the mouth? Deviation to the side can give the sound a noisy quality, as in pronouncing an *s*, which produces a lisp.

Critical to efficient functioning of the structures of articulation is an understanding of how muscles around the mouth function and how the jaw relates to the skull and larynx. Knowing how the mouth and jaw function will give you a way of evaluating voice and speech problems that relate to articulation. A brief look of the skeletal features of the head is necessary for a better understanding of this area.

AN OVERVIEW OF THE ANATOMY OF ARTICULATION

Your jaw, lips, and tongue are some of the busiest structures in the body. Since they are heavily involved with both talking and eating, they are in use much of the day. As in the pharynx, the structures of articulation play a dual role in the digestive process and in speech. The action of the muscles that are used in speaking or singing differs greatly from their action in chewing and swallowing. When the two get confused, difficulty for performers can arise. For example, inexperienced vocalists often "chew" their words. The intricate control of tongue and lips needed for the sustaining of sound demands careful practice on the part of the performer.

In practice, the interaction of the articulatory structures and the rest of the vocal tract is such that it is practically impossible to separate them. However, learning about the correct functioning of these structures will help both performers and those who work with them to understand the whole picture better.

Bony Structures of Articulation

The bony structures associated with articulation are the skull—particularly the temporal, sphenoid, maxilla, and palatine bones (together these last two bones form the hard palate)—the mandible, and the hyoid bone (see figure 6.1). These bones act as fixed or stabilizing factors for the muscles used for articulation.

It is worth spending some time examining the anatomy of the jaw because unbalanced movements in this area can seriously affect articulation and tone quality. Figure 6.1 includes the bony structure of the temporo-mandibular joint. Note that the part of the mandible (the condyle) that forms a joint with the skull has to move forward on a rounded hump on the temporal bone. For this reason, the movement of the mandible is slightly forward and down, not just downward. Many performers have the habit of pulling the jaw down to make vowels and consonants. This is evident when opera singers, especially males, overopen the jaw to emphasize a dramatic point. Anatomically, this puts strain on

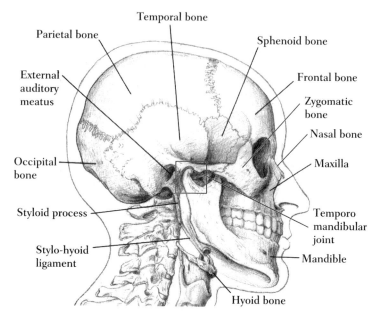

FIGURE 6.1
Skeletal structure of articulation

the joint and surrounding area and thus interferes with good vocal sound. Anytime the mouth is overopened, it makes it difficult for the tongue to reach the teeth to form the consonant needed. Furthermore, such an exaggerated action tends to close the back of the throat (pharynx), the area that needs to expand most for resonance.

MUSCLES THAT MOVE THE MANDIBLE

The muscles that move the mandible are some of the strongest in the body because they are used for chewing (see figure 6.2). The muscles of mastication include the temporalis, masseter, and medial and lateral pterygoids. These are all extremely powerful muscles, and between them they are responsible for

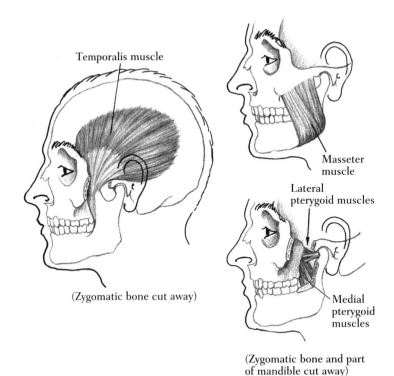

Temporalis muscle

(Zygomatic bone cut away)

Masseter muscle

Lateral pterygoid muscles

Medial pterygoid muscles

(Zygomatic bone and part of mandible cut away)

FIGURE 6.2
Muscles of mastication

five types of movements of the mandible: up and down, forward and back, and side to side.

Observing Changes in Sound with Different Positions of the Jaw

Here is a way to feel the actions of the jaw and at the same time hear what a difference in sound small changes of position can make. Do not exaggerate these movements; a little goes a long way. If you put your fingers in your ears, you can feel the movements easily.

With a partner sing or speak with the jaw in the following positions:
- forward
- backward
- clenched
- deviated to one side
- loose and hanging freely

The temporalis, masseter, and medial pterygoid elevate the jaw and keep your mouth closed unless you are talking or eating. The temporalis originates from the temporal area on the skull (parietal bones) and inserts on the coronoid process of the mandible. If you look at the temporalis carefully, you will notice that it is fan shaped and that the fibers not only go up and down but the ones toward the back slant toward the back of the skull. That part of the muscle is, as a result, capable of retracting, or moving the mandible backward.

The masseter muscles are the ones that form a visible lump when you grind your teeth. These muscles originate from your cheekbone, or zygomatic arch, and have multiple insertions along the whole ramus (or perpendicular wing) of the mandible.

The combined symmetrical action of the medial and the lateral pterygoids causes protrusion of the jaw, and alternating action of the left and the right muscles produces grinding and chewing movements. The action of the combined lateral pterygoids is to pull the mandible forward slightly just before opening the mouth (see figure 6.2).

Notice that in the above discussion very little is said about muscles that depress or lower the jaw. Although the lateral pterygoid can begin the process of opening the mouth, it is the letting go of muscles like the temporalis and masseter and the pull of gravity that allow the mouth to open farther. With the exception of a small muscle called the digastric (located under the mandible), no other muscle is in place to lower the jaw.

Efficient articulation for speech and singing will involve minimal movement of the jaw. Ideally, it will be lightly suspended, flexible, and free to respond to the need of the moment. Any undue tightness, such as clenching the teeth or jamming the jaw downward or protruding, will affect the shape of the pharynx and soft palate, the movements of the tongue and hyoid bone, and indirectly the larynx. And, as you learned in chapter 5, these actions will change your voice quality and your diction for the worse.

Exercises for the Jaw

What follow are some exercises to keep you from clenching your teeth or overopening your mouth, and to help you open your mouth without deviating the jaw to the side. In the process, these exercises will also give you clearer diction. Again, find a partner or use video feedback for confirmation of the benefits.

1. Sing or speak with the tip of your forefinger between your teeth near the front on the side. Do not open your mouth any more than that. This will keep the jaw from interfering, from either overopening or clenching, and allow the tongue to be flexible and the soft palate to lift. It is common for singers to substitute extra jaw movement rather than to lift the palate. When the jaw overworks, it prevents the tongue and palate from doing their jobs. Note: performers singing at the top of their range will want to open the mouth a bit wider than is indicated

here. However, overopening is not necessary in order to sing high notes.

2. To help with the problem of clenching the jaw, open the mouth wide and massage the area just under the cheek-bones near the ears where the muscles attach. You may even find that area sensitive. Do this before beginning a passage and in the middle of the piece as well. The jaw will begin to get the idea that so much tension is not needed.

3. Use a mirror to make sure your jaw is centered as it opens. You can help this by placing the tip of your tongue centrally just behind your upper teeth and moving the jaw up and down, without moving the tongue away.

MUSCLES THAT FORM THE LIPS

Anatomically, the lips are part of the muscles of facial expression. In general, these muscles lie just under the skin, attach to skin, and have few or no bony origins. If these muscles had bony origins in the way that other muscles of the body do, you would get very little movement of the face. When we are communicating face to face, a large part of the brain is busy taking in all the subtle signals given off by the person speaking. If you want to test this, look at a movie that has been dubbed. Even if you know the dubbed language, you will find it almost impossible to understand, because the lips and sound are not matching. The brain becomes thoroughly confused when the eyes and the ears are getting different messages.

The lips are made up of a confluence of several muscles of facial expression (see figure 6.3). They include the following: the elevators of the upper lip and corners of the mouth; the circular

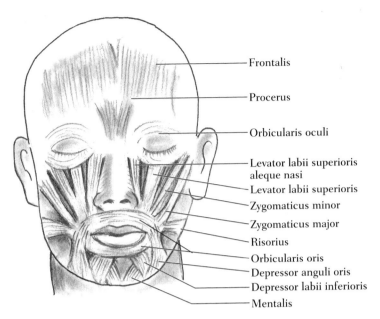

FIGURE 6.3
Muscles of the lips and facial expression

orbicularis oris, which closes and protrudes the lips; the depressors of the lower lip; the retractors of the corners of the mouth and lips; and the muscle on the chin, the mentalis, which protrudes the lower lip. The muscle that has the longest name of any in the body is part of this group: the muscle of the upper lip alongside the nose—or levator labii superioris alaeque nasai. The names of the muscles of the lips tell you the actions.

Movements of the lips will obviously change the configuration of the anterior part of the vocal tract. When the teeth are covered, the lips dampen the sound, much like a mute placed in the bell of a horn. Tense lips will pull on other muscles and have a domino effect in the upper pharynx. Overly protruded lips tend to pull the back of the pharynx forward, limiting the space needed for resonance.

Exercises for the Lips

When your lips are stuck to your teeth or pulled in, they dampen the sound, like a mute on an instrument. If they are tense, diction and rapid articulation of words become nearly impossible. With a partner or video feedback, sing or speak text while doing the following:

1. When your lips are tense, put your hands gently on your cheeks and push the lips *slightly* forward to get them away from the teeth.
2. Make sure that the lips go forward rather than into a tense smile position when pronouncing *ee* as in "meet."
3. Keep your lips loose and flexible by gently placing a fingertip between your upper lip and teeth while practicing.

THE TONGUE AND THE MUSCLES THAT FORM IT

The tongue is a fascinating structure, bigger than you think, because a large part of it is out of sight, and capable of many movements. It has muscle attachments to the skull (styloid process), the hard and soft palates, the mandible, the hyoid bone, and a very small slip of muscle to the superior constrictor of the pharynx. The larynx sits just under the back of the tongue and is elevated and pushed up under the back of the tongue when there is tongue tension or during swallowing.

The tongue plays a major role in shaping vowels and consonants. It can thus be either an asset or a liability in voice production. Its movement can completely reconfigure the vocal tract, depending on the degree of freedom and flexibility, or of tension, that is involved.

The muscles of the tongue fall into two main classifications: the extrinsic muscles, which connect the tongue to other structures, and the intrinsic muscles, which are tiny slivers of muscle that are located inside the tongue and run through the extrinsic muscles. The extrinsic muscles are responsible for gross movements such as protrusion or retraction of the tongue; the intrinsic muscles are responsible for subtle movements and can help you do things like form grooves or turn the tongue over.

The extrinsic muscles of the tongue are paired and include the following (see figure 6.4):

"Glossus" means tongue.

1. The genio-glossus is a muscle that forms the bulk of the tongue. It originates in a small area on the inside of the front of the mandible and has three bundles that form a fan from the front to the back of the tongue. These muscle bundles act together to protrude the tongue: separately, they can also draw parts of the tongue downward.

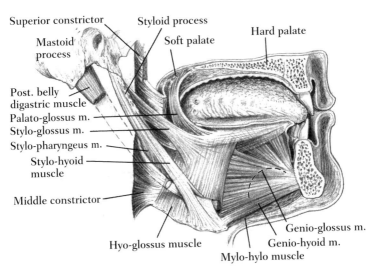

FIGURE 6.4
Muscles of the tongue

2. The hyo-glossus is a flat, ribbonlike muscle that originates along the length of the greater horn of the hyoid bone and inserts into the back of the tongue. When this muscle contracts, it pulls the tongue down in the back. Some dialects have this as part of their pattern, which is difficult to change for performers. The hyo-glossus can also act as an unwanted antagonist to the soft palate, because if the back of the tongue is pulled down, the soft palate will be pulled down with it.

3. The palato-glossus muscle originates in the underside of the soft palate and inserts on the sides of the tongue at the back. Because both the origin and the insertion of this muscle is soft tissue, the movement would depend on which end was the most stable at the time.

4. The stylo-glossus originates from the styloid process on the skull and runs along the under edge of the sides of the tongue all the way to the front. This muscle draws the tongue back and up during the initial stages of swallowing.

There are four pairs of intrinsic muscles: superior and inferior longitudinal, transverse, and vertical. These muscles vary from person to person, and actions such as grooving or turning the tongue over are considered to be hereditary. However, this is not an excuse for an inflexible, poorly used tongue in performance.

Below are some exercises that will help you with tongue movement and flexibility.

Exercises for the Tongue

The first exercise is really child's play; and you probably did it as a child. Making crazy faces and making funny sounds with your tongue can still be valuable for voice professionals.

1. Use a lot of lip trills ("raspberries") and tongue trills ("motorboats") on a wide range of pitches in your warm-

ups. Challenge yourself and do both of these together. It is possible, but you may need a towel.

2. Place the tip of a finger gently on the center of your lower lip. Now every time you finish a consonant or word, make sure that the tongue returns to the front of the mouth by touching your finger. Think of having a lollipop there. This exercise keeps you from tensing and retracting the tip of your tongue so far back in your mouth that it cannot be available for good diction.

VOWELS AND CONSONANTS

The tongue, soft palate, and lips do most of the work of articulation. Their movements create changes in the vocal tract that give rise to resonances we recognize as vowels. Each vowel has a slightly different configuration (see figure 6.5). For example, to produce an *ee* the tongue is high in the back, for an *oo* it is slightly lower, for an *ah* it is usually at its lowest. As you move from what are called closed vowels, such as *ee, ay,* and *eh,* to the open sounds of *oh* and *ah,* the tongue gets progressively lower, resulting in a different configuration of the vocal tract.

Ideally, the soft palate is raised to allow optimal vocal tract space and resonance for all but the production of nasal sounds and consonants. You can watch the action of the soft palate by standing in front of a mirror and saying *ah* followed by a nasal *an.* To see even more, visit one of various speech and phonetics internet sites that have videos of the vocal tract in action.

Consonants are made mainly with the tongue and lips. It is the actions of the tongue as it touches the soft and hard palate and the teeth and of the lips working together that produce consonants.

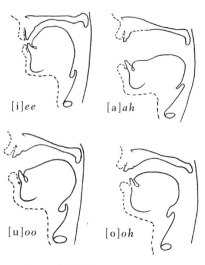

FIGURE 6.5
Vowel shapes

The jaw plays less of a role than you may think, only needing to close with consonants such as *j* and *ch, sh, s,* and *z*. The exercise using the finger in the teeth will have demonstrated that.

Consonants are classified according to how they are physically made and whether they are voiced or unvoiced (see figure 6.6). If you can sing on a consonant, it is voiced. If you cannot, it is unvoiced. Sounds that have nasal resonance are *m*'s and *n*'s, while *s*'s and *z*'s have air escaping and are called fricatives.

Sometimes childhood speech patterns continue into adulthood. One of these is the pronunciation of some sounds on the side of the mouth. These might include the *s*, where the tongue deviates to the side, the substitution of *f* for *th*, when a person uses the lips instead of the tongue to make the sound, or simply the deviation of the lips to the side to make the consonant. If you find you pronounce any consonants such as *s, v, th,* or f to the side, stand in front of a mirror and make sure there is no deviation of the lips or the tongue to the side. You can find words to

Physical action	Examples	
	Voiced	Voiceless
Upper and lower lips	b. m*	p
Upper teeth and lower lip	v	f
Upper teeth and tongue	th (thing)	th (this)
Alveolar ridge (just behind teeth) and tongue tip	d, n*, l, z**,	t, s**
Alveolar ridge—palate boundary and tongue blade	z (seizure)	s (she)
Hard palate and tongue blade	j	
Soft palate and back of the tongue	g	c, k, q
Glottis (opening between vocal folds)	h	

* Nasals   **Fricatives (noisy, escaping breath)

FIGURE 6.6
Classification of consonants

practice by writing out a list of those that give you trouble or go through the dictionary and practice all the words you can find that have those sounds. A good speech and language therapist can be very helpful in solving problems of articulation.

HABITS OF ARTICULATION THAT ADVERSELY AFFECT THE VOCAL TRACT

As we have noted before, there are many ways to alter the shape of the vocal tract. Some habits involving the tongue persist in many performers. Armed with this information, perhaps you can avoid some common traps.

1. Pulling the back of the tongue downward inhibits the ability of the soft palate to move upward.
2. Excessive tongue tension, which causes the larynx to be pulled upward, closes off the oral pharynx and also prevents

the flexibility needed for rolled *r*'s and quick movements needed for rapid speech and singing.

3. Pulling the tongue downward, in a misguided attempt to make more space, pulls the pharynx forward, the palate down, and the larynx up.

4. Overopening or jamming the jaw downward making it impossible for the tongue to articulate with the teeth and palate (basically obliterating the consonants).

These habits can be corrected with good alignment and a free neck, face, and jaw. Practice in front of a mirror, and make sure that you remain flexible and produce sound easily. This challenge is very worthwhile.

IF YOU LOOK NORMAL, YOU PROBABLY SOUND NORMAL

Close observation of a performer's jaw, tongue, and lips will give many clues to problems of voice quality. It is possible to know how people sound by observing what they are doing with their faces. They will sometimes distort their face in order to make their sound, as heard inside their head, fit their voice type.

By looking at a typical amateur choir, you may get a good idea of facial expression and accompanying sound quality—the sopranos may have an exaggerated smile and an overly bright sound, the altos may cover their teeth with their lips to help darken the sound, the tenors may show the head and chin tilted upward, as if to reach high notes, and the basses may dip their chins into their chests in order to sound lower. Many times such habits derive from a person's effort to sound like his or her perception of a particular voice quality. The result is distortion of some part of the vocal tract and resonance, loss of message, and reduced quality of the performance.

Careful attention to pronunciation of vowels and consonants is imperative for good communication. Nothing is more frustrating for an audience than not understanding the words. If your message is important to you, you will do everything possible to make it clear. This may mean practicing in front of a mirror to ensure that your facial expression matches the message of your text.

Summary of Part I

Part I has taken you on a brief journey of the vocal mechanism. Now you have a more solid basis for understanding your instrument and an increased awareness of how it can serve you best when you treat it well.

Good alignment is the first step to having an efficient vocal instrument and an important aspect of your confidence and image. Check it at every opportunity until it becomes part of you.

Being able to take a breath without thinking you need enough to last for the whole day will enable you to trust that your brain knows how much you need for phrasing in practice and performance. A deep breath, rather than a big breath, will enable you to sing, perform, and live your life more calmly.

The larynx, pharynx, and structures of articulation are all subject to poor habits of speech and faulty perceptions of vocal production. These areas function well in singing and speech when the body is aligned and flexible and when the perceptions of the performer do not override the natural intelligence of the body.

There is one exercise that seems to bring all these areas together and give the performer the sense of using the whole instrument well. It is described below.

Exercise for Coordinated Vocal Production

The Alexander technique teachers call this "the flying monkey." Anytime I have used it, it has produced an efficient, aligned body and voice. Always go through these steps in order.

This exercise has to be done in four steps (see figure SI.1):

1. Bend the knees deeply without changing any other part of your posture.
2. Bending at the hips, move the whole spine, from head to coccyx, parallel to the floor. Think of the head going forward and the buttocks going backward. The face is looking at the floor. Be sure that you are bending at the hips and not anywhere else along the back.
3. Raise your arms parallel to the floor and level with your ears.
4. Now sing a song or recite a dramatic dialogue.
   In this position, the head, shoulders, chest, and hips are beautifully aligned; the legs are not able to influence the torso, because they are bent; the breath support is automatic; and the vocal tract responds to the sound without effort. Practice in this position to get the sensation of efficient vocal production. Then gradually return to an upright position maintaining the feeling. If at any point along the way you lose the sensation, return to the original position.

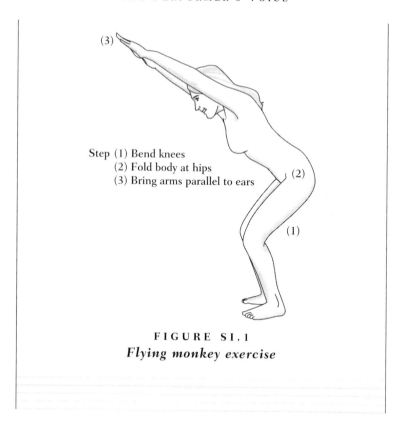

Step (1) Bend knees
     (2) Fold body at hips
     (3) Bring arms parallel to ears

FIGURE SI.1
Flying monkey exercise

Never forget that the physical mechanism is only a part of the picture. By having explored the ideas and exercises in this section, you now are in a position to make further discoveries about yourself and others. However, as with most things, the more you know, the less you know. Making artistic and pedagogical assumptions on the basis of inconclusive scientific evidence will limit your ability to explore and perceive.

Use this information as a first step to knowing and perceiving more. Voice research has come a long way in the past twenty years, but it is still in its infancy. While it would be nice to have more definitive knowledge about vocal function, we do not. This is the nature of science. Exploring is part of the excitement. When we explore with expectations, we limit the possibilities of what can be discovered.

Therefore enjoy the new knowledge you have gained, and respect that which you learned before now. The quest for knowledge is a process that never ends.

PART II

The Art of
Vocal Expression and
Presentation

Part II of this book asks you to consider how effectively your message is being delivered and whether it is achieving its target. Chapter 7, "Vocal Color and Expression," discusses the elements that make a performer expressive; chapter 8, "The Art of Presentation," is an acknowledgment that at some point in your life you will have to speak in public—and very few performers are really prepared for it. What better place than a book on voice to learn how to do this.

Words and language developed as a way of describing pictures and feelings. Today we have become involved with the words to such an extent that the pictures behind them have been neglected. For performers, those pictures must be fully there every time they communicate. Every word has an inherent meaning, and expressive artists convey that meaning when they perform. Too often performers go through the words and/or music without any consideration of the color needed—as if just uttering the words were enough. Audiences deserve more than that. A fully expressive, colorful voice comes from a number of factors:

- your energy
- your physical connection and coordination of your vocal instrument
- your passion for the performance, song, or topic
- your perceptions, background knowledge, and sensitivity regarding the subject
- your imagination and the life in your eyes

Although vocal expression can be practiced, it is ultimately the spontaneity of the performer's relationship with the text that delivers the most convincing message. The factors listed above are a must for the successful communicator onstage in any circumstance. Without these things in place, the balance of the communication becomes skewed toward the words, and the important nonverbal aspects are not present to help the message be persuasive.

7

Vocal Color
and Expression

The ability to express yourself freely onstage is the key to excellent communication with your audience. The audience knows when a performance is convincing. The performer knows as well; she feels a unity with the audience. The balance of physical, emotional, and mental energy, and imagination needed onstage comes with practice and experience. Inexperienced performers often compensate by being over the top with energy or by appearing too casual. They may have seen some of many professional productions and speakers that seem to depend on excessive levels of energy rather than on quality of performance to impress their audiences. This amounts to cheating the audience. Not only is it often the result of misconceptions about what constitutes a performance; it also betrays a lack of deeper understanding and working with the text. The depth with which you approach the text can make all the difference to the quality of your performance. Begin by asking yourself some questions about your text.

Beginning to Think about Preparing Your Text

These are just a few of the questions you will have to answer each time you work with a text. They are important no matter what language you are using. If you are singing or speaking in a language that is new to you, or one you do not know well, you will have to work even harder to produce believable diction and satisfy your knowledge and curiosity about the words.

1. How much do you really know about your text? Do you understand every word?
2. Can you describe your character and every other character in the scene? Chapter 11 has a further exercise specifically for developing your character(s).
3. Do you know the psychological makeup of your character?
4. What is the physical setting? Is it inside or outside? What are the specifics relating to the setting: the colors, materials used, shapes of things, plants, animals, trees, atmosphere, and so on?
5. If you are a singer, have you learned the text without the music? (This will be discussed in part III.)
6. In general, what specific information do you use to establish your character?

The area of vocal and artistic expression is one where the performer can be completely misled as to how much is enough. The tendency for beginning performers is to give not nearly enough. They truly believe they are being credible. Faced with a video of the rehearsal or performance, however, they are amazed to find out how bland it can be and what habits they have that interfere with the message. Rehearsal is the place to experiment and be daring, not to hold back. To save all of your expressiveness for the real performance is extremely risky. Performances and expression have to be practiced. Get in the habit of playing, and having fun, with your sound from the very beginning.

In addition to your physical energy, working with words and ideas creates the emotional and psychological impetus to trigger your imagination and give color and meaning to your performance. Your physical energy was discussed in part I. It is worth repeating, though, that unless your vocal instrument is fully aligned and efficiently engaged, and your breath flowing, it is very difficult to deal with expression. The body, voice, and text all need to express the same idea at the same time. This balance defines a fully congruous message.

To know generally that the character is in love is fine, but it is not satisfactory for compelling performance. Your imagination has to be much more involved than that. Playing with words and ideas is a good place to begin.

PLAYING WITH WORDS

The sounds that give the voice resonance and carrying power are vowels; consonants supply definition to the words and character to the vowels. The vowels are often cheated in text work and in singing because they are not given the full time they merit. They get mixed up with the consonants by being chewed or distorted by excessive tongue and jaw movement, and the flow of sound is impeded. To get used to the idea of voicing on the vowels, you might intone, chant, or even sing your text. To begin you can use one pitch that is comfortable for you. Explore your vocal range on the vowel sounds of your text, and, for the moment, let the consonants become secondary. Below are some exercises to get you started.

Exercises for Playing with Text and Sound

Exploring your vocal range by elongating vowels and playing with consonants is useful for developing an expressive voice. These exercises are also good for freeing the voice. Anytime you feel you are becoming too tense while rehearsing, do this with your text instead. You will find it a welcome relief for you and your voice. First emphasize the vowels, then move on to voiced consonants like *m* and *n*.

1. Intone your text as if it were a sustained chant.
2. Play with the vowel sounds in all the words of the text. First singsong the words. For example:
   Whoooo iiiiiiis siiiiiiiingiiiing thaaaat soooooong?
3. Using the same exercise, vary the range and pitch with each new vowel sound as illustrated below.

FIGURE 7.1
Vowel waves

4. Experiment with adding voiced consonants (see chapter 6 for definition) such as *m*'s, *n*'s, *s*'s, and *v*'s in an exaggerated manner. All of these consonants need some sound, so it will not be difficult. Go through the same exercise and add triple consonants in front and behind all the elongated vowels. It is much easier on voiced consonants like *d*, *v*, *l*, *n*, *m*, and *z*.

5. Now try to make the same effort with unvoiced sounds like *b*, *f*, *k*, *p*, *t*, and *ch*. If nothing else, you will have a good laugh at yourself.

ADDING PHYSICAL EXPRESSION TO THE WORDS

Physical expression is an interesting aspect of performance. In an opera or stage production, it is part of the expectation. Regarding other performances (particularly classical song recitals) and public speaking, by contrast, there are some fascinating perceptions and misconceptions about how we express ourselves. When you look around at people in normal conversation, you will see them being very expressive physically. Their bodies are animated, and their hands are appropriately expressing the words or emotions of the moment. Put those same people in front of an audience, however, and the expression disappears. Preconceptions about performing, self-consciousness, and outdated ideas tend to create this inhibition onstage. In the field of singing, the suggestion that a singer in concert use his hands to help express the text often raises eyebrows. Physical expression that is appropriate to the circumstance and text appeals to audiences and offers them a chance to connect with the performer. Audiences warm to and love classical recitalists who dare to use physical expression as part of their performance. It is easy to forget that the audience is there to be involved. Not using your hands at all looks almost more abnormal than using them too much. The fear that the expression will be exaggerated keeps many a stage artist from communicating adequately. The words to remember here are "appropriate to the text and the situation."

Observing Physical Expression

You can learn a lot by watching people communicate with one another and an audience.

1. Observe normal conversation between friends or colleagues.
2. Watch children express themselves, and listen to the wonder and exaggeration in their words.
3. Ask yourself how successful the communication in numbers 1 and 2, above, would be if people were not using any "body language," especially their hands.
4. Are there any physical mannerisms that impede vocal expression or vocal technique? An example might be excessively raising the shoulders to express emotion.
5. Are there physical habits that give the text a meaning different from the original intention? For example, is the person/performer constantly furrowing her brows for everything she says, including nice or happy subjects?
6. Notice how an audience reacts when a performer brings appropriate physical expression to the stage.

If you observe carefully, you will notice that some physical expressions are inappropriate. The inexperienced performer must be acutely aware of this danger, because it can seriously interfere with the vocal technique and change the vocal quality. Always check that the body is in good alignment, that the shoulders are quiet for both breathing and relaying the words. With such alignment, the message will come from the whole performer and have a profound depth and meaning.

The exercise below enhances your expressivity by combining mental imagery with physical motions. It makes sure that your verbal message and your physical message are saying the same thing. While you might not want to use this exaggerated version in performance, you will find that your text is much more expressive and that the vocal color is built in for you. When you do want to add more physical expression, it will be appropriate to your text and message, rather than hands that just need to do something.

Developing Physical Expression and Encouraging Your Imagination

When developing appropriate physical expression, work in pairs or videotape yourself. Observing someone else or watching yourself in action can be an eye-opener. Remember, how you think you look and sound and how you actually look and sound may be very different. This exercise is designed to build a convincing, expressive performance one step at a time.

1. First choose some text or a song with a lot of character. You may even use a children's story for this exercise. However, if you do, follow the same principles for a text you are performing later.

2. Perform this piece (in good alignment) with as much expression as you can, and without any obvious physical use of the hands for now.

3. Repeat the piece, and give any character, whether human or animal, a completely different voice—as if you had to be all the characters in the scene because there were no other actors there. These voices can be in different ranges and indicate different ages, such as those of a very young girl or a very old woman.

4. Repeat the exercise once more, keeping all the changes from steps 1–3. Now you need to add miming with your

hands to the text. Add hand motions that make pictures for the appropriate text. For example, for a text about going down a long road where there is a big house, as you speak or sing, you use your fingers to demonstrate walking, extend your hand to your side to show the length of the road, and outline the size of the house with both hands. For your information—miming can be done with serious and nonserious messages.

At first, exaggerate all that you have been asked to do. Although it may seem very strange to you, it provides a way to break habits of unhelpful movements and substitute ones that match the text.

After you have completed the exercises above and watched yourself doing them on the video, go back and notice people in normal conversation. After all, you are having a conversation with your audience. How over the top were you in the video? How different was your vocal expression? If you find that your vocal expression is dramatically better but that the hands are a bit too much, remember to use the same vocal expression without using the hands as much. Ideally, you will find your way to having an expressive conversation with your audience.

PLAYING WITH YOUR IMAGINATION

Most of the exercises and observations in this section are simply ways of triggering pictures in your own mind. They are here to remind you that you had this ability as a child and that it is still useful. Playing "pretend" is a good way to enjoy yourself and stop being so serious in practice and performance.

The examples and exercises given above had a visible physical component. Physical movement influences the imagination, and the imagination, influences physical response. There is no one correct way to approach expressiveness.

The exercise that follows is very subtle, yet can make a big difference in your sound. You may feel the difference but not hear it for yourself. Work with a friend who can give you feedback, or with a video.

Making Sound All over Your Body

In this exercise you will be imagining sound being produced in different areas of your body. Although by now you know where sound is produced on the physical level, you will find that imagining sound coming from somewhere other than your mouth can make subtle changes in its quality and color. You may have to do each exercise a number of times in order to shed your old patterns of thinking about sound. Let your partner or the video camera do the listening as you do each thing. Don't try to analyze and perform at the same time.

1. Pretend your mouth can move into different places in your body, and perform your piece in each of the following areas:
   - your head
   - your heart
   - your solar plexus
   - your pelvis
   - your back
2. What differences in the sound for each area do you or a partner notice?

3. Perform your piece thinking of sound coming from mouths located in every pore of your body at once. What happens then? Do this a number of times to get the feeling of it.

You may want to consider each of these areas according to the character you are portraying and deliberately choose a center for that role.

PLAYING WITH IDEAS: USING SUBTEXTS

Actors learn to improvise by using subtexts, and adding their own dialogue to the text, as a rehearsal technique. It would help all performers to do this.

Singers take note! This means using your text as a starting place and improvising additional dialogue in between the actual lines of the text.

It takes time to master this, but it is worth the effort in terms of characterization and aiding your memory. It is great fun to do it with songs. You have to be willing to treat it like child's play. Of course, the normal rhythm will be interrupted, as will the music. The following example uses the poem "Mary had a little lamb":

Mary had a little lamb—
Now Mary is a very pretty little girl. She wears a pink dress with a white pinafore over it. She has blue eyes and the nicest smile.
little lamb little lamb

This lamb was the tiniest of all her lambs. When it was born, Mary
fed and loved it so much that it thought she was its mother.

Mary had a little lamb, whose wool was white as snow.

You have never seen such a coat of white—all soft and fluffy.

Everywhere that Mary went, Mary went, Mary went

Believe me, Mary went to town. She traveled by bus and even
walked long distances.

the lamb was sure to go.

That crazy little lamb went too. It was not about to leave Mary by
herself. There's no telling what she might do if left on her own.

This represents a very simple kind of subtext. No doubt when
you get your imagination in gear, you can do better than this. It
is a great tool for acting, singing, and giving talks as well.

PLAYING WITH PHRASES AND SENTENCES

Every conversation and every text has its own rhythm. Listen to
any conversation; at times the words just tumble out, and immediately thereafter they may become slow and intense. When a
performer grows too serious and heavy-handed with the words,
they all tend to begin to sound the same, and it is difficult to find
the ends of phrases and sentences. This is particularly true of
public speakers who may be trying to monitor their words at the
same time as saying them. Only robots and computers speak
with completely even words and sound. As humans, we do not
want to sound like that.

Singers need to know the rhythm of the text separately from
the setting by the composer. Sometimes one sentence can
occupy several pages of a score. It is easy to lose sight of where
you are going.

Giving Impetus to Your Text and Music

This exercise gets you moving verbally and physically. You can do it alone. However, it is easier when you have a large room in which to do it.

- While reciting or singing your text, and walking very briskly, move across the room until you come to the period at the end of a sentence. At that point your walking comes to a complete stop. You then take a breath and continue doing the same until you reach the end. This will help you feel the movement of the sentence.
- When you can feel the whole sentence, go back and pause slightly for commas.

PLAYING WITH MUSICAL PHRASING

When you hear wonderful performances of music, you often want to dance. For inexperienced performers, however, it is easy for the music to become stuck because they have to think of so many things at once.

Exercise to Keep the Music Moving

For this exercise it is best to use a large black/chalk board in a classroom, and you will need two pieces of chalk and a lot of space. It is a wonderful way to practice runs.

- Take a piece of chalk in each hand.
- Use your hands interchangeably to draw your phrases and melodic motifs as you sing.

The end result will look something like a poor version of a Jackson Pollock painting. But the object here is visible movement of the music.

IT PAYS TO TAKE RISKS

Taking personal expressive and emotional risks is an important part of learning to be expressive. Working with expression is fun, especially when approached like child's play. This is the time and place to leave your analytical mind behind, let your imagination run wild, and simply enjoy the moment. The more you can do this in practice, the more likely it is to happen in performance. Explore, experiment, and play first in front of a video camera. Become satisfied only when that performer in the video looks and sounds genuine. You will know your boundaries and be in charge of your ability to be expressive in public.

8

The Art of
Presentation

Many times a performer will walk onstage, look wonderful, and then open his mouth to speak. This is the moment when the audience will mentally choose to stay or to leave. It is too easy to think that the singing, acting, or great words will suffice, or that any speaking you do will be overshadowed by the music or the drama. You cannot afford such thinking. Every minute you are in front of the public, you are performing, and ideally everything you do will be of a consistent, excellent standard.

Whether you are giving a formal lecture before a concert, an informal introduction to a new work, or a summary before a voice jury, teaching, or giving a conference lecture, you need to know how to be convincing before an audience. Your "public" can be as small as ten or as large as a thousand. The important thing to remember is that you will be successful when you are interesting, engaging, and involved in your subject. Speaking without these criteria is a waste of time for you and your audience. Just as in any other form of performance, be fully present and willing to be there. If you are speaking in public, it is for a reason—you are there to share your information.

Performers are used to being onstage and playing roles. When you speak for yourself, though, rather than for a character, it can become nerve-racking. According to opinion polls, one of the things that strike the most terror in men and women is to be asked to give a presentation. Most people become weak in the knees or self-conscious and suddenly feel the need to be perfect. In a millisecond their personal power is freely donated to an audience that is given credit for being able to see every wart, spot, or error. The self-critic becomes the one giving the presentation, and we forget that it is okay to be human. The woman who was at home in her personal space suddenly becomes a stranger who is self-monitoring and apprehensive. Audiences do not expect perfection; they have come to hear *your* message. They deserve an enthusiastic, energetic person who is dedicated to and consistent with his or her message—a person who really wants to be there.

In a skilled performer or speaker, presentation is a continuation of good communication skills and is visually, vocally, and verbally congruous. It is concerned with rendering a message that is far more important than you personally. Every time you become aware of yourself, or wonder what your audience is thinking, the message has been forgotten. Everything you say and do must match that message, or it will become distorted in the minds of your audience. Self-consciousness, gestures that have nothing to do with the message, pacing without a purpose—all create conflicting information. Ideally, the message and you are as one. When this happens, the performer/speaker is captivating, and the audience remembers.

Observations about Speakers You Have Seen and Heard

Think about your favorite speakers and how they perform in public. By choosing what you like best in them, you can develop an excellent model for yourself.

1. What are the characteristics of the speakers you like? The speaker can be a teacher, professor, fellow student, or experienced public presenter.
2. What are the physical things that you notice about that speaker?
3. Is his or her use of hands appropriate, or does it display nervous habits?
4. Do the eyes indicate that the speaker is in contact with the audience?
5. Are you absorbed in the speaker's message?
6. Are the words and the nonverbal messages of the body and the voice in balance rather than in contradiction to one another? An example of contradiction might be hands that demonstrate something short when the word "long" has been uttered, or someone talking about being calm and yet pacing or fidgeting at the same time.

Faulty perceptions about what constitutes a performance or a presentation, and particularly formal occasions, are at the root of 90 percent of the problems relating to appearing in public.

You are a human being sharing with other human beings

The perception that formal means being perfect and delivering the perfect talk causes the person onstage to lose confidence and to rely on memorization or reading—both of which are deadly and can easily bore your audience.

When you memorize a talk, you can become overly sensitive to going off script. As soon as you make even the tiniest slip, a little voice in your ear shouts FAILURE. The audience may have no idea about what you noticed. The self-critic then takes over, and that renders it difficult to be involved with the message. It is virtually impossible for the inexperienced speaker to react or respond to the needs of the audience with a memorized talk. Unless you are a fine actor or have been specially coached, reading a speech is a poor way of being interesting. When in doubt, be your best self.

One of the most common errors in preparing a public talk is that of writing it out as if it were a piece of literature. When a talk is written and edited as very correct prose rather than as the way people normally speak, it is difficult for the audience to follow. If you want to test this for yourself, have a friend read part of a textbook aloud to you, and see how much you can retain. This literary approach to preparation is usually worked out in one's head—and then on paper—and is generally a complete surprise to the speaker when he hears himself read it for the first time, probably at the event.

If you are going to write out a speech, present it to an imaginary audience, and write it as you speak. Then practice reading it in the same way. Ideally, you will not need a complete text, unless it must be given as a specific class assignment, for a business report, or to the press. Even then, a spontaneous introduction and summary would help considerably.

DEVELOPING A CREATIVE, SPONTANEOUS PRESENTATION

A creative approach to what you offer your audience will include variety, interest, and substance for listener and speaker alike. You are there to entertain, inform, or educate. If you want some ideas for creative performance, go to a concert directed by Bobby McFerrin. He has the performers and the audience, and anyone else he can find, singing, moving, competing, and, in general, having a wonderful time. He does not seem to have any rules for formality for his concerts—and no one complains.

Passing on useful information is similar to good teaching. An outstanding teacher will offer knowledge in such a way that the students want to listen and to participate. Depending on the size of your group, this can take many forms—anything from straight delivery to brainstorms, discussion groups, and group artwork relating to the theme. Know that you have many options, and dare to use some of them. Organizing your approach and thoughts on the basis of wide-ranging choice will enable you to mix and match ideas spontaneously in your presentation.

We do not write and speak in the same way, and it is important not to confuse the two approaches. Think back to times when you discussed a subject with friends and colleagues in comfortable, casual circumstances. Were you at a loss for words or a way to describe the information? And, when they did not understand, you probably were able to describe issues in several different ways. The thought of giving the same information as a "presentation," by contrast, immediately conjures up concerns and thoughts of inadequacy. The key to spontaneity and creativity is feeling at home with your information in whatever space you occupy.

Exploring Your Topic

Before you organize your presentation, play with your information and explore your topic from a variety of different angles. This will enable you to have enough information to vary your topic and to improvise when necessary. This exercise is useful for anything from a five-minute talk to planning a long seminar.

1. Broaden your perspective before you narrow it. Almost every subject you can imagine has its own set of in-house jargon and preferred definitions, and unfortunate assumptions are made regarding the audience's understanding of these. The best way to alleviate this problem is to pretend you have never heard of your topic.

2. Look up the key word, and its original derivation, in a large dictionary and begin a mind map of all the words that are given. Remember that this key word is your topic, not necessarily the title of your talk. Do not edit out any words or ideas at this point. Accept what you see. If you use a word like "vocalization," be sure you look up the root word, "vocal or voice," as well. You may well come up with a few surprises and some thought-provoking definitions during this exercise.

3. After you have exhausted the dictionary definitions, think of all the associations—good, bad, or otherwise—you might have with your chosen word. Add these to your mind map. Do not forget any sayings or phrases that come to mind. This part of the exercise is best done with a group because each person will have his own associations and memories. You might also ask your friends and

colleagues what they think the word means. The diversity of opinions will astound you. They will all have different definitions according to their own perceptions and experience with the topic. The more you broaden your concept, the easier it is to come up with multiple ideas and options.

4. Now add any emotional words associated with your topic. While you may not think emotion is relevant to your topic, you will find that others have pleasant or unpleasant experiences to share. In fact, many varied emotions surround any topic.

At the end of the exercise above you will have a page full of words. If you wish to group them under major headings or topics, do so. You may have a subject that contains modifying words, for example, "vocal expression." Think of ways these words might modify your main topic of expression. Include the most important of these words now. However, do not start to plan your talk yet. Before beginning to work on your talk, answer the questions below.

Focusing on Main Points

Before you can prepare a successful presentation, you need to determine what you want your audience to know. Asking the following questions will help you focus on your key points:

1. What one thing do I want my audience to remember and take away? The answer to this question can be a fact, a value, a concept, or the creation of trust or credibility for you, your school, or your business. Unless you have an

answer, you will not have a focus for your presentation. Remember that your answer has to be informed as well by your knowledge of the people in your audience, who they are, and why they are there.

2. How much can people remember? You do not want to leave them with information overload and indigestion. If you have five minutes, one main point is all you can make. The maximum for any talk is five major headings—and still only one focus.

3. How clear is my data? Even though you live with your data all the time, you cannot expect an audience to decipher it as quickly as you. If you are using visuals, keep charts and graphs simple and key items well marked or colored. Anything complex is best put on a special handout to be distributed after you speak.

4. How do I show my main point(s) on a slide or overhead? Remember that most people store information in pictures and are visual. A simple picture or a cartoon is thus very helpful. A picture *is* worth a thousand words. Make sure that your important items can be seen a split second after a slide is shown. When your audience has to look to find or follow the information, it will not hear what you are saying. In other words, make points blatantly obvious. The performing arts are these days experimenting much more with visual backgrounds and pictures to enhance the concert. Make sure that anything you use truly fits the message of the concert or drama.

Having spent some time with all your newly created ideas by using definitions and associations, you can now think about organizing your materials. Generally, there are three parts to a presentation: an introduction, the main body of the talk, where you develop your ideas, and a summary or benefits section to finish. This structure can be compared to that of a musical composition with exposition, development, and recapitulation. In fact, many recitals today are being organized around themes. The above ideas will help you to think through the various texts you are using and to organize them into an interesting concert.

THE INTRODUCTION

The introduction serves only one purpose—to get your audience interested in listening to what else you have to say and to establish the focus on your issue or topic. It does not need to be a list of the topics to follow—far from it.

Look at the words on your mind map. Do they suggest any stories, experiences, or real-life situations that would serve as a good introduction? Your introduction can be varied infinitely. It can be a story, a personal related experience, or a one-word brainstorm with the audience that sets the stage for what comes next. You may choose on the day of the presentation to change your introduction. When you have done the preparation as suggested in the "Exploring Your Topic" exercise box, you will be able to make the change easily.

The introduction is the time to create common ground. You do this by relating first to the human beings in the audience. Then you present the people your information—not information to the people. Think for a moment where your emphasis is. Is it on data and facts, or is it on your audience and their needs?

Pitfalls and words to avoid in introductions include these:

- I would like to talk to you . . . (just do it).
- I am going to talk about . . . (again, just do it).

- I hope you will . . . (weakens).
- Telling jokes that have nothing to do with the topic.

There are no throwaway lines. When you say, "Good morning, ladies and gentlemen," you must mean it. When you include a greeting, look at your audience, not your notes, and mentally give them time to reply.

‿ *In order to create a pause, you can repeat your greeting silently to yourself.*

BODY OF THE TALK

Now that you have people interested, give them specific information and detail. Return to your mind map for the organization of appropriate concepts and headings.

There are various ways of presenting the ideas in the body of your talk: role plays, mini-dramas, simple, direct presentation, in-depth brainstorming or discussion groups, or questions and answers specific to the issues you want discussed. You must decide whether you wish to talk or to facilitate. The more you are able to allow your audience to take part, the more it will own the topic. Refer back to the discussion of how Bobby McFerrin manages a concert. However, facilitation requires careful planning and the ability to respond quickly and to think on your feet. It demands flexibility and spontaneity.

Be adaptable enough to be able to shorten, lengthen, or rearrange the order of your points. The audience's survival and yours are not dependent on getting every word that you have planned to convey. Be observant of the needs of your audience, and change the pace or direction when necessary.

THE SUMMARY

This section can be powerful, persuasive, or gentle, depending on the message you choose to deliver. It is useful to include benefits and emotional comparisons like "people who use these techniques are less nervous and enjoy their performance," "performers who follow these guidelines will save themselves time and energy and the performer will be vocally healthy," "the way to keep your audience happy is to . . . ," and so on. You may repeat your main message. For example, "If you take only one idea away with you today, I would like for it to be. . . ."

Finally, you will improve your preparation by talking over your ideas with other people first. Find out what makes sense to friends, family, and colleagues. Talking about your material clarifies it in your own mind and allows you to know when you are too complicated. You may find what you thought was clear in your mind sounds disorganized when stated aloud.

Whether you are giving a lecture in vocal pedagogy or a conference paper, the above principles will help you deliver a substantial, organized message. Those of you who perform lecture recitals or poetry readings with explanations can be adventurous with your material as well. Examples, interesting anecdotes, and appropriate shared experiences, funny, happy, or sad, will be interesting to your audience. It is not just information you are giving out; you are sharing an experience as well.

DELIVERING YOUR TALK

After you have decided on the primary message and purpose of your talk, you can make some choices about how to present the material. This is determined somewhat by the size of your audience, the kind of atmosphere you wish to create (casual, serious, and so on), the available equipment, and seating and platform arrangements. Ask questions about these things ahead of time so that there are no unpleasant surprises. Do not be afraid to request the arrangements you want.

When you know your material well, do it with few or no notes. You may want to have a brief, one-page outline, or reminders for your eyes only on your computer presentation, to keep you on track. Ideally, the introduction will be completely spontaneous. For the rest of your information you may use notes, cards, slides, or pictures. Be sure you get to your venue early to check the setup, your slides, computer setup, overhead, proper pens, and the like. More important, you want to get a feel for the space and make it your home.

USING VISUALS

Putting important points of your presentation on a slide or overhead is useful, especially for a conference, a paper delivery, or a preconcert lecture. The *visual* majority of your audience will appreciate this. Wherever possible, think in/and or use pictures. Out of this may come some clever ways to put across your ideas.

One of the most creative ways we have to deliver information today is computer-generated presentations such as PowerPoint or Keynote. The scope and possibilities are endless for pictures, animation, music, and so on. There are uses for these tools in concert to provide background and atmosphere for the music or for doing something really different for scientific and business audiences. Sadly, most often, the computer is not used in such a creative way, because doing so takes skill, a great deal of thought, and planning. Just to put ordinary words and information in a computer presentation is to lose a creative opportunity to deliver a significant message to your audience.

Unfortunately, in the business and scientific communities, the common practice is to put words and complicated graphs on PowerPoint or slides. Have as few ideas as possible on one slide (perhaps three or four main points). If you pack too much onto the slide, the audience is so busy trying to read it that it is not available to listen to you. Remember this in a performance as well. There is more experimentation with visuals in the performing arts. Some of it is wonderful. Do not, however, use anything that will divert the attention from the performer. Simplicity is the key.

Some speakers use their slides as keynotes for memory. This is acceptable as long as they do *not* read each word and sentence to the audience, whose members can read for themselves. It is better for you to explain why those points are there and the specific information related to them. The objective is to maintain a spontaneous, flexible, and comfortable format. Trust your knowledge; you do not need to read the slides.

INTERACTIVE PRESENTATION AND FACILITATION

The skill of interactive presentation lies in making it easy for your audience to respond. Think of the excellent performers, teachers, and speakers who interact with their audiences. To them it is a very natural thing to do. For the inexperienced, it will seem like a very big risk. It could well be the happiest risk you ever take. The value of interaction is that it gives your audiences an opportunity to share the stage, and the responsibility of doing some work and for thinking for themselves. Also they are more likely to own or share the outcome.

Brainstorming

When you want to find out quickly what the group is thinking, use a one-word brainstorm. You can do this with small or large groups and in a number of ways.

⌒⌐ *How you word your question(s) for the brainstorm is extremely important. The more specific your question, the more closely the answer will meet your objectives.*

For example, you might ask your listeners to give one word for their association with classical music or with Shakespearean drama. Their responses can furnish you with plenty of talking points.

During a brainstorming session be sure that you include each person and accept every word offered. You can also add your own. If your listeners do not come up with one of your key words, put theirs up first and then suggest the one word they did not think of, or ask permission to add yours. You are in charge of the discussion, so you can choose the words that are key to your message to move further into your presentation.

Small-Group Discussion

Done well, discussion groups will create your presentation for you. Sometimes it is nice to let them do all the work. Your job is to oversee, accept what they have to offer, and shape the message. This takes careful and thoughtful planning. Getting the response you want will depend directly on the way you present the questions or issues and your clarity about the outcome you want.

Issues or questions that are too general will generate too many ideas and lack focus. For example, the question "What are the problems in your school relating to communication?" could generate many answers, a lot of negativity, and no steps to a solution. Here's a better way of presenting the issue: "What are the three main issues relating to communication in your school? What is working well at the moment? What problem areas need immediate focus? Come up with three ways of improving these areas."

READING A PRESENTATION EXPRESSIVELY

Sometimes it is necessary to read a presentation. In that case there are some helpful suggestions for being expressive. Reading a presentation tends to inhibit the freedom and range of vocal expression, particularly when all the words and phrases are read at the same rhythm and pace. It becomes difficult to find the important points. Expressive reading requires a great deal of rehearsal and planning.

If you tend to jot down a presentation hurriedly, discuss it only in your own mind, or depend on a computer-generated template for a quick way out and then read it, you stand every chance of boring the audience. If you are not sure what it is like to be a recipient of such a *read* presentation, have a friend read part of a formal essay to you. It is likely to have little or no spontaneity or normal speech quality in it.

Remember, when delivering talks from a script, to practice your presentation aloud many times before you give it. Here are some ways to do that.

Reading with Expression

If you have to read a presentation, you must build expression into your message and rehearse it thoroughly. Here are some steps that will help you engage your audience and retain its attention.

1. Underline all the important words you would like to emphasize.
   - Go through the script a second time, and choose the most important words.
   - Now look for the most important ideas, and mark them in some way.

• Read aloud, emphasizing all the words you have underlined.

2. As you rehearse or practice your presentation, walk your phrases as suggested in the exercise box "Giving Impetus to Your Text and Music" in chapter 7.

⌒ *This will help you get a sense of the rhythm and pace of the words and the breath. It will also move the words to the end of a sentence without your dropping your voice. Many phrases begin with a strong, firm voice, only to disappear at the end.*

3. Rehearse the talk as if you were a ham actor going completely over the top. You will not do this in the actual presentation, but it is a very good rehearsal tool.
4. Review the exercises in chapter 8 for vocal expression. The exercise using the hands to tell the story is particularly good.
5. Use a video camera to record your practice. This feedback could be the most important aspect of your practice.

Remember that your ultimate focus is your message. When the speaker is focused on the message, so is the audience. When your mind is elsewhere, so are the minds of your listeners. It is your responsibility to make your audience want to hear more or to follow up on what you have said. Your listeners are not supposed to attend a course on listening first. Your energy and involvement in the subject will stimulate them to pay attention.

COMMON TRAPS FOR THE
INEXPERIENCED PRESENTER

The listener who is not stimulated very quickly reverts to his own thought patterns and personal concerns. He is no longer there. Anything about a presentation that establishes a repeated rhythmic pattern will put him to sleep. Here are some examples of such unhelpful patterns in a presentation.

AN EXCESS OF SPECIFIC INFORMATION

Inexperienced speakers and teachers tend to want to tell an audience everything they know, leaving no space for listeners to absorb the material. Even when listeners have a focused mind, it is difficult for them to take in the vast amounts of information contained in excessive data, lists, or complex graphs. This kind of presentation indicates that such a speaker is unsure of the message and therefore has tried to include everything. Too much information causes verbal indigestion, overwhelms the brain, and frustrates the listener. The result is the mental loss of your audience.

Think of information like a kind of food gauge—really more like a full or empty stomach. When you are on empty, you are uncomfortable. However, when you are full, at that moment you never want to see food again. The same is true of verbal or information overload. The fill factor is best at about 75–80 percent. That way your audience will have space to know whether it wants more information or will want to go away and read your materials.

THE APOLOGETIC PRESENTER OR PERFORMER

You never need to apologize for being onstage or for giving a presentation. It is not part of your message, and it sounds as if you were preparing the audience for a poor performance. People are there to hear your message, not your excuses. We have far higher expectations of ourselves than the audience does, and it is usually the self-critic who is apologizing. The only time it is appropriate to apologize is when something unavoidable arises spontaneously during a talk or performance.

Um's and Er's

Extraneous sounds occur because the speaker has a warped sense of time and feels the need to fill in the gaps in sound. For the presenter time goes slowly, and any silence can seem endless. It is okay to be silent. Your audience will not go away. Those silent periods, usually lasting seconds, give your audience time to catch a breath and allow your information to sink in.

The new computer voice recognition systems apparently have trouble understanding extraneous sounds, and they are creating havoc with dictation. Who would have thought that computers would improve our ability to speak?

Ineffective Use of Hands

We use our hands comfortably and naturally in everyday life. However, when we think we have to keep them still, we tend to develop extraneous twitches of hands, heads, shoulders, hips, and feet as substitutes for using them in a talk or performance. People who live whole days, weeks, and months without thinking once about what to do with their hands become worried about them when faced with a presentation or a performance.

Hands are part of the visual aspects of your presentation. As long as they move in tandem with the messages and words you are using, they are fine. Your hands do not need to remain fixed in one place for the whole time you are onstage. They look perfectly normal hanging by your sides or used expressively and with purpose. Frozen hand positions look far more awkward than use of hands to express the message. If you are worried about this, record your presentation on video so that you can see for yourself.

TIMING YOUR TALK

Experienced speakers and classroom teachers know how to keep to a schedule when presenting. They have learned just how much time they need for the amount of information they wish to relay. Inexperienced speakers can find timing difficult. For them, timing, speaking, or reading the talk aloud is an essential part of the preparation.

If you are reading your presentation, you can easily time it. A single-spaced page of text read at a reasonable pace will take approximately two and a half to three minutes. Taking less time will indicate to you that you are reading too fast.

Speaking with notes or slides is more spontaneous and thus more difficult to time. A rough guideline is that a twenty-minute talk ideally will have about five to seven slides and no more than four main points.

Most audiences will love you if you finish your presentation early, but the opposite may happen if you run over. When your presentation goes beyond your allotted time, you become extremely unpopular with your audience, the next speaker, and the organizers of the seminar. Even if you think that every word you have prepared needs to be delivered, your audience does not. It has lost interest and concentration at this point. It is much better to stop short, do a quick summary of the material you are currently presenting, and cut to the end of your presentation.

When you are unsure of your timing or afraid that you will go over, ask a friend or colleague in the audience or the person in charge of the event to signal to you when you have five minutes remaining. That way, you will not be surprised and caught without enough time to close your presentation in a logical way.

LAST-MINUTE CONSIDERATIONS

Presenting yourself well and receiving feedback and acknowledgment from your audience is an exhilarating experience. First-time actors and singers, and sometimes teachers, find themselves on a real high when they experience the wave of energy that flows from the audience. Speakers have the same experience and grow to love the interaction with audiences, large or small.

Giving Your Presentation

When the moment comes to give your presentation, you must be mentally engaged and physically grounded. Here are some essential things to remember when giving your talk.

1. Remain focused by thinking of your center as being located three fingers below your navel. Breathe in and out of that area and support your voice from there. Deep, well-supported breathing is essential to dynamic vocal delivery.

2. If you are using a microphone, remember that it is there purely to magnify the sound you put into it. Using a microphone is not an excuse to produce a flimsy, unsupported voice. Your sound must be energized and expressive before you ever reach for the mike.

3. While you are speaking, plant your feet on the floor. Grounding is important for your energy, nerves, and voice. Nervous feet take away energy and power from your voice. Move only with a purpose—for example, to

get to the slides or flip chart or to talk to someone specifically. Mindless pacing distracts your audience. When you and your message are integrated visually, vocally, and textually, you will not distract the audience.

4. If you lose track of where you are or make a mistake, pause for a moment, take a deep breath, and let your audience know what has happened. It is sympathetic and probably aware that something is causing you discomfort. Your acknowledgment of the situation will help put you and your audience at ease.

Giving a presentation, whether formal or informal, is, after all, a performance—a sharing of your information with your audience. You are not talking at people or trying to give them "information indigestion." No talk, about any subject, ever has to be indigestible or boring.

WHAT TO DO WHEN YOU MOMENTARILY LOSE CONFIDENCE

Presentations or performances are rarely, if ever, perfect. Knowing this is the first step to remaining centered when something does go amiss. Rather than panic when something does not go according to plan, the first thing to keep in mind is that you will probably be the only one in the whole auditorium or room who knows it. If you do encounter a momentary glitch, take a deep breath, and continue. Remember that time is going slowly for you and fast for your audience. Listeners are most likely to perceive your momentary stop as a pause and welcome the chance to catch up with you.

When Murphy's law is in full force, there is little you can do except improvise. However, when in doubt, err on the side of simplicity. Do not attempt to read large amounts of data to an audience. Instead, describe the picture you were planning to show or tell a story around the data. Your presentation may be far more spontaneous and better than you planned.

If it is your first public talk, practice many times beforehand. Giving a first performance of any kind is likely to be nerve-racking. If you are totally calm, you will probably make history as being the first ever to be so. The best way to allay fear is to practice a lot and visualize being at ease on the day (see chapter 11 for a thorough discussion and exercises). Every time you have a negative thought or picture of yourself onstage, replace it with a picture or thought of how you want to be on the day. Practice talking aloud in front of a mirror; have conversations about your subject with willing friends and colleagues.

It is normal for the actual performance or talk to come out differently from your rehearsal. Trust the process.

Remember that you are speaking because you are sharing your knowledge. You would not be there if the subject matter were not within your scope of competency.

When you do not know the answer to a question, say so. Bluffing your way through invites far more embarrassment than saying you do not know. Offer to find out the answer or to send that person to someone who is knowledgeable in that area. Remember that you are not omniscient and that being human is okay.

When a question is irrelevant, quickly find a nice way to ask the questioner how it applies to the information in your talk. If he can apply it, clarify the question; if he cannot, tell him that you will be happy to discuss it with him later. Make a point to see him after the talk so that he will not feel neglected.

Very rarely is the audience, or anyone in it, your enemy (and this includes audition panels and voice juries). This, however, is often the perception. When you expect an audience, or anyone else for that matter, to be an enemy, you are setting up a negative situation that invites negative reaction. Make friends with your listeners, respect them and their knowledge, speak positively about your subject, and be a good listener when someone takes issue with what you have said. Involve them in the process by asking them questions and making them think. This is the best way for information to be shared and owned by everyone.

CREATING A COMFORTABLE SPACE FOR YOU AND YOUR AUDIENCE

Presentation or a spoken performance is an art when you can make people feel comfortable listening to you. Being a gracious host or hostess to your audience is the same as entertaining them at home. When you feel at home, so does the audience. Be just as enthusiastic as you would be in talking with friends. Your enthusiasm shows your interest, and your passion for the subject allows the audience to be included in your personal relationship with the topic.

Create space for the audience to absorb and understand what you are saying. It needs time to see, hear, and experience the information you are conveying. By keeping the information simple, you make it easy for your audience to absorb what you are saying. Put complicated subject matter in simple form on handouts, where people will have a chance to read it over and over when they do not understand it, or to think about it more carefully at a later time.

Absorbing oral information is difficult, so be considerate of your audience when planning your presentation. Remember the "food" gauge. Leave them wanting more.

In short, always present your best self, devoid of habits that interfere with your message. Practicing your presentation does not mean that you cannot be "you" in public. It is an important step to developing spontaneity and comfortable delivery. The variety and color of your voice is fully available to you through your imagination and dedication to your message.

Summary of Part II

Being expressive and comfortable with your material is a requirement for excellent performance. When both you and the audience feel that you are sharing the life of the characters or information created by you, it is energizing and exciting for all. While it is not so useful for you to become too involved emotionally, the audience loves to laugh or cry with the situation and the character. Allow it this pleasure.

You now have many tools for increasing your vocal color and expression. Although you may have to work at it to overcome your own self-consciousness, you will gradually give yourself permission to take necessary and appropriate performance risks. By constantly monitoring your practice with a video camera, you will be able to be your own best coach. That is not to say that teachers are not useful. On the contrary, a good teacher/coach is considered essential in the voice world. Still, you can do a great deal for yourself. It will aid your work with your voice professional and give you added confidence for performance.

Whether you are performing set repertoire and/or giving a talk, be equally professional in your preparation and planning of both. Planning a lecture-recital, spending all your time on the recital, and neglecting the speaking part, will ruin the event. Likewise, designing wonderful visuals and graphics and then presenting yourself poorly will destroy your message. Learning to deliver all of your material is the first step to introducing and selling your ideas in a genuine and interesting manner.

PART III

The Art
of Performing

Performing in public can be exciting and satisfying. The energy you get from what you give, and what you get back in return, can create a buzz that lasts a long time. When you perform well, the satisfaction is immense for you and your audience.

Performing well involves a balance of creativity, spontaneity, and knowledge of basic, healthy vocal principles and of keeping your voice healthy. This balance is so important because it is likely that much of your learning has been dedicated to analytical-critical thinking and data-specific information. The best performers learn to balance the intellect with feeling, emotion, and intuition. The left brain is usually in charge of intellectual thinking and the right brain in charge of intuition and spontaneity. An effective performance requires a balanced use of intellect and intuition. This balance will give you the opportunity to allow something special to happen while performing.

For the purpose of this book, performances are not limited to the stage but are more broadly defined to include auditions, interviews, debates, competitions, and exams. These all need to be prepared and envisioned like any public performance. Presence begins when you walk in a room, not just when you are onstage.

9

The Ingredients
of Performance

The best vocal artists are risk takers. They are not afraid to lose control in order to gain it. Students and would-be performers who dare not do something, because they think it might look or sound silly, must develop the ability to allow change and experience something new in order to become good. Allowing yourself to say, "What would happen if I did it this way," and taking personal perceived risks will make it easier for you to be flexible in the performance situation, especially when other people like conductors and directors are involved. An attitude of exploration and experiment is essential to your ultimate success.

PRINCIPLES IMPORTANT TO YOUR APPROACH TO PERFORMING

How you approach your performance can make a big difference in the outcome. Basic ingredients of effective performance include a positive attitude, focused practice, including a practiced "performance," objective feedback from others—as well as your own awareness and self-monitoring—and reliable and healthy vocal technique. When you approach performance with these essential ingredients in balance, you will experience the freedom to relax and enjoy it.

BE POSITIVE

Preconceptions about what it means to perform often get in the way and stop you from opening your mouth to make any sound in public without criticizing it. These preconceptions include everything from ideas that only highly trained singers and actors perform in public to self-judgments about the quality of your voice as heard from the inside rather than the sounds heard by the audience. Somehow, when there is an audience, performers feel the need (it may be subconscious) to be absolutely perfect—even when we are just being human most of the time. The first step to a tense performance is the idea that performing has to be perfect according to your standards, rather than fun and enjoyable.

Being positive about performing means using a positive vocabulary. There is increasing evidence that positive thinking and the vocabulary you use set you up to succeed. Words and phrases like "I am capable of doing this," "I can do this," or "I will do my best" will create an atmosphere in which you can reach your potential.

Unhelpful words that are best eliminated from your spoken and mental vocabulary include "right" and "wrong," "should" and "ought," "control" and "hold." These words inhibit spontaneity, creativity, and intuition, and they set up in our brains an internal radio of nonstop comment and negativity. These and many more thought forms tend to lower the immune system temporarily. Discard such thoughts, and reward yourself for positive, helpful, and nonjudgmental thoughts and language.

PRACTICE "PERFORMING"

Get in the habit of performing for just yourself and your mirror or video camera, even when learning. It is not wise to save it for the stage only—that is too scary. Improvise by doing crazy things with your text as suggested in part 2, be a "ham" actor in front of the mirror, make up tunes and create mad operas to your texts, even if music is there already. When you improvise, there are no "wrong" ways of doing things, because you are creating the melodies and using your imagination with text. Practice differently every time. This way you learn to be flexible and have fun at the same time.

This advice applies to singers and speakers alike.

INVITE FEEDBACK ABOUT YOUR PRACTICE AND PERFORMANCE

Never be afraid to ask for advice or clarification about your performance. Healthy curiosity can be very constructive. Listen carefully and give the person you asked the right to his opinion. It is not helpful, however, for you to give all of your power away to someone without knowing for yourself how you have done. The best way to know this is to use a video camera to film your work and your lessons. It is very important that you see for yourself how you are doing. That enables you to work together with your coaches or teachers rather than have to accept what they have to say just because they are the teachers. Respect, cooperation, and coresponsibility for learning are all part of being a good student and performer.

SPEND TIME ON YOUR TECHNIQUE

When people speak of vocal technique, it is easy to assume that it means the physical function of the voice. However, by now you will have discovered that how present you are, how well you are seeing, and how you use your imagination are all part of what is considered "vocal technique." The mind-body connection is important to good technique.

A healthy vocal technique is considered basic to good vocal performance, whatever the style and situation. Pop and classical singers alike need an efficient, reliable technique that gives them confidence as well as vocal health and longevity. Many performers, particularly classically trained singers, have been criticized for becoming so involved with the technical aspects of vocal production that they forget about the message in the words and music.

Audiences do not want to watch a singer *sing* or an actor *act;* they want to become involved and be part of the meaning and emotion of the performance. Vocal artists who are thinking about how they are making sound while in front of an audience are not really performing. When the technique is there and completely at the service of the message, truly magical moments can occur. A reliable technique provides the ease and freedom for your imagination and creativity to capture the audience. When you concentrate too much on your voice and how you sound, the message that comes across to the audience is "I am being very diligent about my voice." The message of the text and/or the music is then lost, and the audience becomes bored very quickly.

CREATE A VISION FOR YOUR PERFORMANCE

Performing with ease requires physical comfort, acute awareness, a vivid imagination, and personal enjoyment. This begins with your own vision and focus on what you want for yourself in performing and what kind of atmosphere you wish to create for the audience.

It is important for you to know how you wish to be perceived. Have you ever spent time thinking about the kind of voice you want to have? If you do not know, neither will your audience. Begin this process by asking yourself two questions: "In the best of all possible worlds, how would I like my voice described?" "If someone heard me sing or speak and were to describe my voice to others, what would I like said about it?" Make a list of the characteristics that you value. For example, this list might include adjectives such as "natural," "effortless," and "expressive." How do you wish to come across, and what is it you want your audience to take away from the performance?

PERFORMING AND VOCAL HEALTH

Vocal ease and vocal health go hand in hand. They are the bases for a long-lasting technique and a beautiful sound. Your technique is the support or the framework for everything you want to do with your voice. Three basic principles of technique have a huge impact on performance: physical balance, breathing, and presence.

PHYSICAL BALANCE

The first principle of healthy vocal performance is good physical balance. Instrumentalists will tell you that the most wonderful technique in the world will not help when their instruments are unbalanced or misshapen. This is doubly true of the vocal performer, whose instrument is the body. It is the equivalent of having a house built with crooked walls on shaky foundations. Those who can sing and speak well, easily, and healthily despite an unbalanced posture are exceptional. Unfortunately, inexperienced performers tend to copy the faults and exaggerations of their performance idols because the poor habits are the ones most obvious to those with limited knowledge. These habits include poking the head forward to project or perform to the audience, holding the body in a stiff and artificial manner, and adopting the super casual, collapsed look.

As you know, how we *think* we look and how we actually look can be very different. Be sure to test for yourself by recording yourself on video. The camera is a powerful tool that cannot be fooled. While feedback from an experienced partner is also very helpful, ultimately, you need to see for yourself to really believe it.

BREATHING DEEPLY

The second principle is that ideal breathing for vocal performance is accomplished silently, easily, and deeply. Notice that the word "deeply" rather than "big" is used. "Deep," in this case, refers to the lower half of your body (including the abdomen and the lower ribs in the back) where you feel expansion on inhalation. You can take in a large amount of air or a small amount, as long as you feel the response deeply in your body.

Ideally, imagine you have a large air channel from your mouth to your lower abdomen. This is obviously not anatomical reality, but by thinking of this depth, you will allow the muscles of the abdomen and floor of the pelvis to release on inhalation. This channel does not change shape during the breathing process, and nothing in the upper chest is disturbed. There is no gasping, no noise that comes from the mouth or throat, and no extra movement of the shoulders or chest. Any visible action of breathing is seen in the lower abdomen and the lower ribs at the back (see figure 9.1). Pay attention to your posture because when the back is overly arched (swaybacked), the lower ribs are not able to respond and it is difficult to get a deep breath. (A thorough discussion of breathing is in chapter 3.)

Many inexperienced performers stop breathing to think. This may sound strange; however, notice what you do the next time you "stop" to think. Mental and physical hesitation can cause us

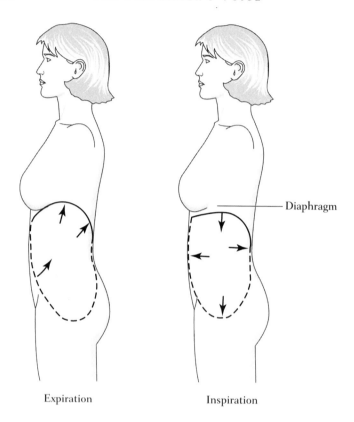

Diaphragm

Expiration

Inspiration

FIGURE 9.1
Action of breathing on lower ribs
and abdomen

to stop breathing for the moment. It's all about flow and, in healthy vocal use, especially airflow. When you gasp or grab a breath, the body wants to lock it in, there is a momentary pause because the vocal folds have closed tightly, the chest has locked, and the voice seizes up just when you want to use it. The breath exercises in chapter 3 will help with the concept of keeping the air flowing.

BE COMPLETELY PRESENT

The third principle is to remain present at all times. Being present implies that you are aware of what is happening around you while you are performing. This awareness does not mean that you will become distracted. Presence is a state of being centered and aware of your personal space, and of having a quiet alertness. In performance, this state acts like a powerful magnet to draw an audience to you. It enables you to be in touch with the music or text, yourself, and your audience. At the same time, it has a profound effect on your physical state and the freedom of your performance. Presence is such an important part of performance that the next chapter is devoted to defining it more precisely.

10

Defining Presence

A performer with presence seems to fill the entire auditorium, no matter what its size. Presence has to do with a sense of space and how to use it. This space is physical and mental and relates to the vision you have of your performing. Anyone with a desire to change and a little imagination can achieve presence. Presence is obtainable. It is a matter of knowing what it is and working at it.

You already intuitively recognize presence; no doubt you take notice when some people enter a room, you know when friends are happy or sad without speaking to them, and you know on which days not to disturb your friends. These are things you sense or feel—often without knowing the reason intellectually. There is something about people with presence and a sense of personal space that exudes a special energy or aura.

Your personal space is your energy field—a portable "home," if you wish—and it has many facets. If those around us can discern it, it must be more than just imagination. A person's presence and his or her use of personal space have a number of visible and invisible factors, which contribute to the whole picture.

PHYSICAL INDICATORS OF PRESENCE

The obvious indicators of a person's presence are posture, energy and health, the eyes, the voice, and levels of awareness and sensitivity. Seemingly invisible factors such as attitudes, thoughts, and imagination contribute equally. In the end, the whole is greater than the sum of its parts. However, by looking at the parts, we can begin to analyze presence and create ways of gaining it.

DYNAMIC POSTURE

Physical alignment and posture contribute to presence and are crucial to commanding space. Balanced alignment and good posture help us look energetic and healthy and contribute to voice quality and the image we convey. A slumping performer cannot physically command space.

Postural bad habits begin early. They are correctable, however, as long as one is willing to cope with feeling strange for a week or two. Change always creates a feeling of not being in one's habitual comfort zone. It is important to remember that the body is full of atoms that vibrate. Posture is therefore dynamic, not static.

Unfortunately, the word "posture" itself tends to be perceived as something rigid or fixed. It would be preferable for you to think of yourself as being flexible, as mobile, and as physically responsive as a cat. Regarding yourself as having dynamic flexibility brings energy and flow to body, voice, and image. Performers with dynamic, flexible bearing and good physical alignment radiate this kind of energy and are magnetic to the audience.

These characteristics are imperative for performers and need to be built into their technique from the beginning of their study.

THE IMPORTANCE OF EYES

Nothing is more attractive than a performer with alive, sparkling, fully present eyes. Such eyes show the expansiveness of your space and your interest in "being here." Eyes with a light in them show life, energy, awareness, and a reflection of a physically, mentally, and spiritually healthy person. Your eyes hold the key to a large amount of information about you. They have served as a basis for diagnosis of physical and mental problems by different therapies and systems of medicine for centuries. Sayings like "The eyes are the mirror of the soul" permeate literature. Many love affairs have begun by someone's being drawn to another's eyes, and many poems have been written to this effect.

It is easy to ascertain a person's presence by the eyes. When you have eyes that are seeing, you are fully present in the moment and ready to listen or respond. Eyes that reflect thinking, feeling, or inner listening are not seeing but appear to be unfocused or roaming inwardly. This can happen when we are thinking about vocal technique, trying to remember the text, looking for an answer, preoccupied with our own internal dialogues and feelings, or busy criticizing a performance as it is happening. For example, watch a performer who is self-conscious. It is likely that the eyes are not really present in the room and neither is the message, because it has been forgotten. It is obvious that the performer is thinking of himself at that moment. When you are "self-centered," you prevent yourself from being fully present, and this is most apparent in your eyes.

The most widely used—and abused—term related to using the eyes is "eye contact." Rarely is this concept defined adequately. Most of us have been left to our own devices when figuring out how to do it. Too often eye contact becomes "eyeball" gazing, and it is extremely discomforting for everyone, including your audience. *Seeing* your audience is very different from staring or glaring at it.

How you see people or your audience is crucial to the way you are perceived by them and is an indication of how you are managing your personal space. When you use 180-degree or a wide peripheral vision to see the people in your audience, they know they have been seen and you have given them a powerful form of acknowledgment. No one likes to feel ignored. Displaying tunnel vision when around people or performing, whether it is simply a bad habit or deliberate, can be interpreted as being cold, aloof, and uncaring toward your fellow human beings or your audience. Everyone needs to be acknowledged, and the simple gesture of seeing those around you or your audience is the easiest way to show it.

Peripheral vision involves using a broad scope of seeing. It is what makes people in an audience think you are performing just for them. Most of us are physically capable of achieving nearly 180 degrees of vision. In the exercise that follows you can test this for yourself. Developing your peripheral vision enables you to see in the context of the whole.

Seeing and looking are two different things. Looking tends to be tunnel-visioned or so focused that one sees nothing. An example of this is a performer's staring at a spot on the wall, rather than seeing the audience. Seeing involves the use of your peripheral vision—the vision that you use when you do not want to miss anything that is happening. Classroom teachers use this all the time. They want to know what children in all parts of the room are doing. They have been accused of having eyes in the back of their heads. You need that same vision and awareness in order to know how your audience is responding, whether it is asleep or needs a change of pace or energy. This kind of visual awareness is important during a performance and keeps you present.

Exercise for Developing 180-Degree Vision

This simple exercise enables you to learn to use your peripheral vision. Knowing what is going on in the space around as you perform can have a dramatic effect on the quality of your voice and your performance.

- Extend your arms straight out in front of you, palms touching.
- While keeping your eyes straight ahead, slowly open your arms out to the side. Notice where your peripheral vision stops. Note how much you can see without moving your eyes.
- While looking straight ahead, describe the detail you see in front, on the sides, upward, and downward.
- Practice this (without the arms) while sitting in rehearsal or walking down the street.
- Sing your song or speak your text to someone in this visual mode. Get a partner to note the difference in the vocal quality and the "look" in doing it this way and with fixed or staring eyes.

AWARENESS

Once you begin to see with a wider vision, your sensitivity is heightened. You are alert to your audience, yourself, and your environment and well on your way to 360-degree awareness. This heightened awareness increases your sensitivity to those around you, sounds, colors, smells, and the quality of the air. You are alert and kept in the present by the millions of antennae around your body that constantly feed you information.

Developing Awareness

Becoming aware of your surroundings is an essential step in enhancing your presence. This is a useful exercise to do while waiting to go onstage or for an audition as well. You can do it when you first begin to rehearse and at various times during rehearsal.

Sit quietly with both feet flat on the floor. Become aware of the following:

- Sounds you hear, temperature, air flow in the room, smells, colors, the feel of the room, the general mood, and the location and activity of other people.
- Become aware of the area outside the room. What things do you sense from that direction?
- Now return to rehearsing.

POTENT INVISIBLE ASPECTS OF PRESENCE

Sometimes it is the invisible rather than the visible attributes of people/performers that define them and their presence more precisely. What is sensed and felt about a person can contribute essentially to personal space and presence. You may think that such factors are difficult to define, change, or improve; but it is in these areas that we redefine ourselves continually as we pursue inner growth and development. They include such things as (1) thought patterns, (2) attitudes and belief systems, (3) our sense of imagination and play, (4) visualization or the ability to change our inner processes to adapt to current situations, and (5) the ability to be true to our unique self. Such factors are critical not only to personal survival but also to compelling performance.

THOUGHT PATTERNS

Learning to live with overly active internal conversations is not easy and definitely not helpful during performance. Such mental hyperactivity puts invisible busy signs on us and inhibits our presence. Your thought patterns are more visible than you think. Just ask someone who knows you well.

There are many meditation courses and systems that devote themselves to teaching people to practice control of their thought processes. Inner stillness is prerequisite to making clear, informed decisions about every part of your life. Thoughts are much like the chatter of a very active internal radio. When we are occupied completely in our own minds, it is virtually impossible for us to observe or listen. Being fully present demands a mind that has space to see, listen, and observe.

A person who has mainly positive thoughts is much easier to be around than someone who is engaged in ongoing internal critical conversation. The positive person fills his or her space with a pleasant atmosphere. Most of us like to be around such people. On the other hand, when you have an overabundance of negative thoughts, you give out a prickly atmosphere and quickly drive people away or make them wonder why they came to see you in the first place. Can you imagine going to a performance where all the performers are being completely negative?

ATTITUDES AND BELIEF SYSTEMS

Thought patterns that are reinforced over a long period of time become the attitudes and belief systems with which we lead our lives. We grow up with attitudes derived from the positive and negative experiences gained from family, cultural, and educational environments as well as the "school of hard knocks." Objectivity is easy to talk about, but difficult to achieve. We all carry a full suitcase of attitudes and preconceived ideas of how we need to function in a variety of situations—including performance.

Having a positive attitude is not only an asset; it expands your presence. The creation of a comfortable performance space for oneself and others demands a positive attitude. Those who do not have it and insist on being continual pessimists drag down the energy of everyone around them, including an audience. Having a positive attitude does not mean believing that nothing negative ever happens. It simply means that you have the energy and ability to deal with negativity or unpleasantness in a mature, responsible manner.

"I want to be here" is an example of a positive attitude. By living this statement, you create an atmosphere that in general encourages openness, sharing, honest discourse—and in performance an expanded and compelling energy field. On a subconscious level, others are as a rule aware of your attitude. It affects them and the rest of the environment. This is doubly so in performance. No matter what is going on in your personal life, during performance you must want to be there.

IMAGINATION AND PLAY

Preconceived ideas about performing often cause us to ignore our most creative and imaginative thoughts. The most neglected gift we have is that of our imagination. What miserable human beings we can be without using our imaginative and creative resources in our performance—no matter how serious the song or topic. Imagination stimulates creativity, curiosity, and a sense of play. Those who can enjoy this aspect of themselves are more likely to be able to laugh with others and at themselves, to be happy, and to be able to succeed in achieving desired goals with ease.

Visualization

Imagination taken one step further becomes visualization. This extremely potent tool is the secret ingredient of success for many people. Visualization is your ability to picture or project yourself into a situation. It is a way of creating your space, programming positive thoughts, creating confidence in a variety of situations, and, in general, programming your mind and body to achieve what you want.

Many top sports personalities consider this kind of training critical to their performance and success. They spend many hours with sports psychologists and coaches working on their mental attitude—seeing themselves having stamina, and doing well, and even winning. Just like those in the performing arts, top athletes constantly have to do their best before an admiring public. Performers need to take a leaf out of the sports training book and do the same. It is a good way to practice your technique and to prepare for public performance, particularly when you cannot get to a practice room when you need it. Silent practice can be hugely beneficial. Performing artists are beginning to learn to use visualization to be more confident and to channel their nervous energy in a positive direction.

How to Visualize

Here are some examples of visualizations that performers will find helpful. You do not need to spend hours doing this. In fact, once you get used to visualizing, you can do it in a split second. However, at first you may have to work with your vision. You do not even need to see it exactly. Just discipline your mind to go over the picture until you get it exactly as you want it. Always replace negative pictures with what you want instead. Once you become comfortable with the idea, develop visions of what will serve you best.

1. Become still and quiet.
2. Choose something technical like posture, for example. Picture yourself standing (or sitting) in exactly the way you will be the most at ease for your performance or practice. You may want to look at examples of good posture before you begin.
3. Visualize or imagine how you want your throat to feel as you use your voice.
4. Picture yourself on the stage or in an audition. See yourself standing well, feeling comfortable in the space— even if you have never seen it before. Now feel the physical ease of your voice, and hear the message, musical or text, being expressed in the way you want it.
5. See yourself creating an atmosphere of performance excellence or an atmosphere where people will want to hear more.

These are only a few ideas. You can visualize the smallest technical detail or a much larger picture. Trust the process. You will be amazed.

Visualization is your way of creating an environment where you are able to do your best. Too often people are busy thinking about all the problems and negative things that can happen. This is tantamount to visualizing these problems and causing them to happen. Seeing what you want to happen is a better way to program your mind and body. It sets up the possibility and probability that it will be a positive experience. We can never guarantee that a performance will happen exactly as we want it. However, we can go a long stretch toward creating a positive event.

In some ways it is similar to programming your mind-body computer. When you are busy visualizing yourself being nervous, inept, and hoping to do well, you are setting yourself up for a negative outcome. You want to create an atmosphere in which you have options as to how you behave and react rather than become caught up in old patterns of nervousness or behavior that is unhelpful.

GENETIC AND CULTURAL FACTORS AND THE UNIQUE SELF

In the best of all worlds, we retain the positive aspects of what we inherit genetically and culturally. These can include a disposition toward longevity and good health, a good physical structure, a pleasant voice, or such things as regional and family speech patterns. They are all to be honored and savored as part of our unique inheritance.

You may give your unique self many names—"persona," "soul," and so on. I describe this part as your core—the spirit that lives in you that no one else has. It is the very thing that makes you human and also makes you a distinctive performer.

PRESENCE: THE EXPANDED HUMAN

Your space is an energy field that you can expand and contract at will. You are in charge of it. You can choose to want to be where you are, stand tall, acknowledge those around you, see rather than look, think positive thoughts about someone, use your imagination and visualize yourself relaxed, at ease, and enjoying what you are doing. It is possible to do this anytime and anywhere. When you are brave enough to do these things as part of daily life, the atmosphere in which you perform changes—becoming more congenial, comfortable, and less stressed. Difficult or stressful situations are treated differently when the focus is directed toward the task at hand rather than toward personal issues.

It often takes a long time to realize that the phrase "human being" is not one word and that the second word is derived from a verb. "Being" creates a comfortable home that can expand at will to accommodate a variety of physical, mental, and emotional states. Think of this home as one that is portable and expandable, and it goes everywhere with you. It is much like your house. However, it is your personal space that can include what and whomever you choose—especially your audience.

Our behavior changes when we feel at home. For example, when friends or strangers have been invited into your home, you become the gracious host or hostess, you are aware of the needs of your guests, you notice whether anyone appears to require your attention, you introduce people who do not know anyone, you know who needs a refill of food or drink, and you know what is happening in other parts of the house. In short, you have optimal awareness; you are on top of the situation in every way and are at your natural best. You are comfortable and in command of your space. Treat your audience this way, and you will find your performance dramatically changed for the better. Become the gracious host for your whole audience, including auditions, and welcome everyone to your performance.

An understanding of your personal space and the ingredients and tools for making it work for you will enable you to create a comfortable home for yourself onstage. Fear, worry, and faulty perception cause this portable home to shrink and atrophy—and your voice to follow suit.

Think of performing in an expandable sphere. You are the dot in the middle, and the sphere can expand to accommodate any size of audience. As you perform, think of filling your sphere with sound, as if sound were coming out all of your pores. Because you will be thinking "surround sound," you will not be trying to aim your voice at your audience. The sound will simply fill space. This will keep you centered and at the same time give your sound a timeless ambiance and presence.

11

Preparation
and Performance

PREPARATION

Preparing to perform is like preparing to participate in a sport. Performing is the chance you have to put all your preparation to use. The mind and the body need equal attention from the very beginning. By beginning with focusing the mind and visualizing what you want, you will alert your body to the need for action.

Preparing to Perform: Observations

Begin your preparation by observing yourself and your surroundings. Having read the chapter on presence, begin to observe yourself and those around you more carefully.

Notice the following:
- What is your own physical awareness of space when practicing and performing?
- Are there others around you who seem to have presence? What are their qualities?

- At what times and in what situations are you most at home in public? When do you feel uncomfortable?
- What happens to the body when someone is happy, sad, at ease, or uncomfortable?
- Do people shrink noticeably when around other people who are perceived to be very important, such as directors, conductors, or managers?
- What are the general awareness levels around you in rehearsal and performance? Are you aware of the times when you are fully present? Are you thinking so much about your own voice that you have no idea what anyone else is doing? When you walk through a room or space, is your internal dialogue such that you barely notice those in your path—or at the sides?

VISUALIZING AND FOCUSING

Visualization was discussed in chapter 10 as part of presence. It is mentioned here again because it is such a vital ingredient of performance preparation. Top athletes and competitors are taught to focus on or visualize their goals before they begin their practice and before every game. This is because it inspires them to reach their potential when it matters most—in performance. Research has shown that good visualization can be almost as effective as actual physical practice. The key to being centered and remaining in the present and in charge of your practice and performance is the ability to visualize what you want to happen. This can include anything from physical elements of your technique to positive attitudes about performance.

The following exercise is an easy way to visualize and focus on the task at hand. Do it at the beginning of every practice session, before every performance, and while waiting or preparing for an audition to center yourself.

Exercise for Centering and Focusing

Here you want to develop a sense of inner quiet, of being at one with yourself and your energy—not rigidity (see figure 11.1). This is a way to begin to get rid of the noisy analysis or the unhelpful inner critic.

With your eyes open . . .

1. Sit (or stand) with both feet flat on the floor. Imagine that all parts of your feet are touching and feeling the floor. Your toes are not twitching or moving.

2. Place your hands on something flat, or on your thighs. Imagine that all the pores on the palms of your hands are touching and sensing where they are placed. Again, the fingers are not twitching or moving.

3. Sit in this complete stillness for at least thirty seconds; one minute is ideal. Become aware of your breath, your pulse, and the inner movement in your body. You may find that you begin to feel a different kind of energy and that your thoughts begin to slow down. Enjoy this strange feeling. It will calm you and enable you to clear your mind of all the inner debris that gets in your way.

4. Observe your breathing. Ideally, you will feel as if you were breathing in air from around your whole body. Deep breathing has nothing to do with the size of the breath or the volume of air you take in; rather, it is concerned with a feeling of depth in the body. Deep breathing at its best is barely noticeable.

FIGURE 11.1
Centering and focusing

5. Visualize yourself creating an atmosphere in which you remain focused and able to do your best in practice and performance.

Focusing on "quietly being" is the first step to readying your mind and body for the tasks ahead. The second step is to get the body moving in ways that will benefit your voice.

PHYSICAL WARM-UPS

Gentle, calm physical warm-ups are better than hyperactivity for the voice, especially at the beginning. The exercises that work best consist of stretches and coordinated movements to free your body and get both sides of your brain working together. Anytime you are doing exercises be aware of your postural alignment.

You can improvise your own physical warm-ups. It is fun to put on some beautiful, slow music and allow your body to move with it. If you are a singer, doing this with the accompaniments to your songs is wonderful. Ideally, your warm-up will include fluid movements, stretching, especially the ribs and spine; exercises that include both sides of the brain, such as movements that cross the midline of your body, for example, cross crawl; and vocal exercises that are fun, easy on the voice, and involving your entire singing and speaking ranges.

Suggested Warm-up Routines

What follows are suggestions for simple physical and vocal warm-ups. They are designed to be easy, fluid, and not frantic or hurried.

General Stretches

Put on some gentle music and allow your body slowly to stretch and physically make the phrasing. Think of the stretch as being created from inside of you, as if the music were inside you creating the movement. You will be surprised how much you can loosen up this way. If you have the music to something you are singing, stretch to that. It will give you a very different feel of the music.

Rib Stretches

The idea here is to give the back muscles, the muscles between the ribs, and those between the rib cage and hips a good stretch. For the best effect, do the exercise slowly.

During these movements make sure the head is over the shoulders and not poked forward.

- Stretch both arms and fingers upward as far as possible. Make sure your head is straight and the arms are parallel with your ears. Reach with one arm and then the other until you can stretch no higher.
- Now stretch both arms forward as you bend from the hips until your torso is parallel to the floor. Push the arms and top of the head forward and your bottom backward. You will look like an L shape with a nice straight back.
- Come up by allowing the arms to lead the rest of the body by stretching them toward the ceiling as you return to a standing position. You will need to use your abdominal muscles strongly to help you up as well. Do not let the head lead.

Keep your arms parallel to your ears and your head aligned with your shoulders throughout this exercise (see figure 11.2).

Physical Exercises for Balanced Brain Function

Cross Crawl

This exercise is similar to marching in place. You alternately move one arm to touch the opposite leg (knee) as you march (see figure 11.3). It is like walking and swinging your arms as you go. You would normally do it using alternating arm and leg (right leg up and left arm forward, then left leg up and right arm forward). As you touch the opposite knee, maintain your good spinal alignment. You may do this exercise while singing or speaking if you wish. However, ten times for each side would be enough.

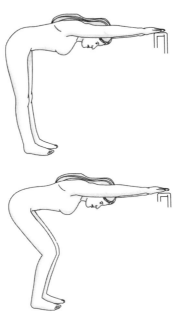

FIGURE 11.2
Rib stretches

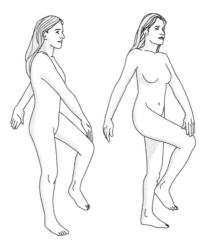

FIGURE 11.3
Cross crawl

Lazy 8's (∞)

This exercise helps you focus and relax the eyes, neck, and shoulders.

Keep the spine aligned and do not lean forward from the waist while you do this exercise.

Begin with both arms outstretched with your palms together, as if you had an elephant's trunk. Draw in the air a large 8 on its side (like an infinity sign ∞) with the arms leading your whole upper body. Begin in the middle of the 8, and move up to either the right or the left to make the pattern. It is important that your first movement be up!

As you draw the 8 slowly, smoothly, and evenly, carefully follow your fingertips with your eyes.

Energy Yawn

Somehow this exercise always helps people use their voices better. You can repeat it anytime your jaw feels tight. If jaw tension is one of your problem areas, do this exercise several times during a practice session or several times during the day. Be sure to keep your head straight over your shoulders. There is a tendency to poke the head forward in this exercise.

Open your mouth as if yawning. While maintaining the yawning position, strongly massage the area near the cheekbone over your back teeth (see figure 11.4). Do this three times.

FIGURE 11.4
Energy yawn

Warming Up Your Voice

Now it is time to give the muscles of your voice some special attention. The vocal warm-ups suggested here do not have to be done as scales or even as singing sounds. By playing and experimenting with sound, you can discover interesting ways of covering a wide range of pitches while relaxing the jaw, lips, and tongue.

Vocal Warm-ups

During all of the exercises below be sure to check your posture, levels of awareness, and presence. Here are some options for you:

1. Lip trills, or "motor boats," going from the middle of your voice and as high as you can go, and then from the middle of your voice and as low as you can go.

2. Sirens up and down—not missing any pitches. This means lots of sliding up and down on an *ng* sound. These will seem like tiny, heady sounds. Enjoy them. They are easy on the voice. As you do them, keep the mouth slightly open. Later you may also use a comfortable vowel sound instead.

3. Tongue trills, or "raspberries," up and down in the same manner as numbers 1 and 2 (this is the same as a continual rolled *r*).

4. Use any of the above methods to practice the melodies of your songs.

5. Using vowels and other vocal sounds, improvise by starting with a rhythm or melody. Just let it develop in any way it wishes to go. Sometimes you can go on and on—especially in the shower. There is no rule that says you must sing or intone anything recognizable for a warm-up.

6. Singing or intoning this or any other text is also a type of warm-up.

When you are using scales as warm-up material, vary the rhythm and beat so that you are not practicing the same way every time.

Athletes have learned never to practice anything the exact same way three times. It causes the brain and muscles to remember the pattern, sometimes incorrectly with faults being built in, and makes it difficult to be spontaneous or react to the present moment. Practicing the same way all the time invites boredom because when you are on automatic pilot, you lose presence and awareness of what you are doing.

Working with Music and/or Text

After you have selected the songs or texts you wish to perform, your imagination will play a key role in learning your music or words and performing. Approach each vocal performance (including a speech) as if you were the director of a play. You choose the characters and know each one intimately (color of eyes, hair, height, weight, type of clothes, etc.), design the set and costumes, and are responsible for choosing every color and piece of material that appears on the stage. When you take this approach, your imagination will supply all the vocal color you need naturally and fill in the picture for the audience. Do this before you ever begin to learn the music. Take the text to each song you are singing, and write a thorough description of each character.

Exercise for Working with Text

Here are some questions to start you thinking and using your imagination with your words.
1. List the characters in the text, including the narrator.
2. Describe the exact physical characteristics of each character, such as color of eyes, height, weight, age, color of hair, skin, and so on.
3. Describe in great detail the clothing being worn.
4. Describe the psychological profile of each character or the person speaking.
5. Describe the setting and scenery in great detail. Determine whether it is inside or outside, hot or cold, what season it is, the details of the building, flowers, trees, grass, water, sky, air quality, smells, and so on.

6. Describe the one message you would like your audience to take away from this performance.

When you have found answers to all of the above, you will be well on your way to an expressive and imaginative performance.

The Words

Your text is your message, and it is important. First learn the words in their own natural rhythm and dramatize them as prose or poetry until they make complete sense to someone else. If you are a singer, do not be tempted to learn the tune yet.

The Rhythm

Every text and language has its own rhythm. No conversation ever has equal emphasis on each word or sound. Each language has its own rhythm as well. Stop and listen to someone speak French, German, English, or Chinese. When people learn a foreign language, it is not the pronunciation that usually trips them up; it is the rhythm of the language. Sometimes words just tumble out, and at other times they are slow or fast, depending on the emotion, enthusiasm, or mood of the moment. In music there is, first, the natural rhythm of the text alone and, second, the basic rhythm set by the composer.

Physical rhythm, or pulse, is the foundation of music and some text. Using your whole body to feel the rhythm is very useful at this point. There is nothing wrong with dancing your song (or text) to learn it.

The Melody

With the words and rhythm firmly in place, you can learn the melody of a song with confidence. Feel the melody and the phrasing by moving your arms and hands to the shape of it. Use a vocally easy syllable such as *pa, la, dee*, or *loo*, or jazz sounds such as *doo-be-doo,* to sing the melody. This makes singing the melody easier and also acts as a vocal warm-up. When you are confident of the rhythm and pitch, add the words.

⤲ *Each language has its own melodic movement. Don't be fooled into thinking that spoken text does not have a melodic line.*

PUTTING IT ALL TOGETHER

By using the suggestions above, you will find that you have built in imagination and expression from the very beginning and are not stumbling or stopping and starting because of inaccurate words or rhythms. This process builds confidence at each step.

FOR SPEAKERS

Preparing to perform is just as important to speakers as to singers, and the same principles and exercises apply. While speakers do not have a specific tune, they need to pay attention to the melody and rhythm of speech and language. The sound of each word has its own sonority and melody (onomatopoeia), and each is a crucial element in communication. Every word you say is important and requires the same imagination as any singer's.

Whether you are a character in a play or giving a presentation, your imagination and enthusiasm are the keys to successful communication. By following some of the guidelines and exercises for singers, you will improve the quality of your speaking voice greatly. Review the exercise in "Developing Physical Expression and Encouraging Your Imagination," chapter 7.

PRACTICING

Consistency and efficient rehearsal are the keys to good performance. A little every day is the best approach to voice work of any kind. Vocal muscles need intelligent and varied repetition for you to create healthy voice habits. It would be ideal for you to spend thirty to forty-five minutes of actual vocal practicing. However, ten minutes is better than nothing. At the beginning it does more harm than good for you to sing longer than forty-five minutes. Practice is thus not something you can do the day before a performance. In fact, waiting until the last minute is not a good option for a confident performance of any kind. It will only lead to a huge case of anxiety.

Singers do not have to be in a studio to practice. They can do much of the work away from a piano or CD player. Visualization can be done anywhere. The words can be learned and recited in any room, in front of friends and colleagues, or while walking. Once you have learned the words and rhythm, you can think or inwardly say or sing your words in rhythm as you walk down the street.

CHECKLIST FOR PRACTICING

1. Spend thirty seconds to one minute focusing.
2. Check your posture.
3. Make sure you are seeing peripherally and are fully aware and present during the entire session.
4. Do two minutes of physical warm-up, using the stretching and exercises suggested earlier.
5. Do five minutes of vocal warm-up, including an easy song or text to use as an exercise.
6. Vary the remaining time between learning new text or music and rehearsing what you know already. It is important vocally and mentally to practice pieces that are at the learning stage, the development stage, and the performance-ready stage.
7. Do some over-the-top miming to get your imagination going. Revisit the "Developing Physical Expression and Encouraging Your Imagination" exercise in chapter 7.

8. Never leave a practice session without singing one song or speaking your text with full involvement with the message, as if you were performing before an audience of thousands. This will get you in the habit of performing without stopping to correct or criticize.

THE PERFORMANCE

Nothing is more satisfying than the supportive energy of a live audience willing you to be wonderful. This is why many performers do their best with an audience.

To perform well, you must put all of your practice and past performances out of your mind and remain completely in the present. There is a danger that you will be tempted to compare your current performance to every one you ever did before, whether in practice or in public. It is common for your perception of your performance and the audience's perception of it to be different. Your audience is hearing it for the first time and is judging you on a limited knowledge. It may perceive you to have done wonderfully; meanwhile, you may place your performance somewhere near mediocre.

Honor the audience's perception of your performance. The best reply to "You were wonderful" is "Thank you." Whatever your thoughts are about your performance, keep them to yourself. The fact is that your listeners know their own taste and appreciation. Respect that! You may well be able to perform the piece better, but an unsophisticated audience may not know that. Your self-criticism does not increase the listener's pleasure or understanding.

We often give the audience credit for knowing everything that is going on inside us when we perform. Many times when performers see a video of themselves, they say, "I was going through hell, and yet I look so calm and in control." How you think you present yourself and how others perceive your performance can be very different.

DEALING WITH NERVES

You want to be confident when you perform. Confidence comes with the process of disciplined practice and attention to learning combined with positive thinking. One way of becoming confident is to pretend you are. "Fake it until you make it" is not a bad adage when it comes to performing in public. This goes along with visualizing success. The audience does not usually see your perceived wobbly legs and knotted stomach.

When people are nervous, it means that they are thinking about themselves more than the message or the music. This is usually the time the words are forgotten. At no time do you want to call attention to yourself by becoming a noisy, active self-critic. Focus on the message of the music or text, and communicate with your audience. By using visualization techniques discussed earlier, you can see yourself on stage or in performance being comfortable, remembering the words, and being fully involved with the message.

PRESENCE

Although presence was discussed in chapter 10, it is so essential to successful performance that it bears repeating here. Your presence is a combination of your physical balance, seeing as you perform, your desire to be there, the text, the music, and the message of the music. Remember that you are sharing this with the audience at all times. You and your sound are the drop that creates ripples going out in all directions so that you fill the entire space.

Developing Presence

Presence is a technique that can be practiced. Developing it is something you can do every day—in your routine activities, in your private practice or public rehearsal, and in all your performances.

- Practice (mentally) expanding your personal space to include those around you. Treat everyone as a guest in your *home*. You can do this walking down the street, in conversation with friends, and in the practice room.
- Sing or speak as if you were the dot in the middle of a circle or sphere. Remember that this circle can surround an audience of five or of five thousand.
- Now extend this concept to rehearsals and then to performance.

THE WHOLE MESSAGE

Part I began by explaining how the voice works and how to use it effectively. It emphasized understanding your body and employing it appropriately to establish a free, easy technique that is so natural that it frees you to concentrate on expression, the message you want to deliver, and the presence to do so in a compelling manner. If the technique is faulty, no amount of presence will compensate for it. There are many ways to approach technique, and you must be ever vigilant to what brings out the best in you.

Part 3 confirms that the message of your performance is complete and satisfying when you are performing with a fully integrated body, voice, mind, and imagination. You can integrate these aspects by knowing what you want for yourself and your audience. Before you perform, ask yourself, "What is the one thing I would like my audience to take away from this performance?" It could be many things. It is up to you to choose one as the "bottom line." For example, "I would like to create an atmosphere in which the members of my audience go away feeling better for having come to hear me." Having an underlying goal for your whole performance will help you to be comfortable with your audience and to believe you have something to offer it.

Never forget that each song or text has its own message. Reliable technique, your careful preparation of the text, your full involvement in its message, and your presence all contribute to a compelling performance.

12

Vocal Health

Your voice and, ultimately, your performance are directly affected by how you treat your body. Your general health and sense of well-being will always have an effect on your voice, so treat your body well.

A performer is a "vocal athlete"; you will perform better if you are in shape. Being in shape comes from appropriate physical exercise, mental focus, good nutrition, and a reasonable amount of sleep. Being an athlete or a performer requires responsibility and wisdom in the way you take care of yourself.

GENERAL HEALTH HABITS

Taking care of your body, and therefore your voice, is as important to good vocal production as developing good technique. It has the added benefit of improving your lifestyle generally.

A POSITIVE ATTITUDE

Numerous studies have been done on the effects of positive thinking on the immune system. It is true that we create our own reality. A positive attitude about your goals, your abilities, your body, and your singing is step one toward vocal health. Striving for perfection is laudable; kicking yourself for not being perfect is a good way to achieve little. Find a way to be positive.

Visualization is an indispensable tool for achieving what you want. It takes no time—only a second to see yourself being able to do what you want to do technically, physically, and for your life.

Meditation is a fine way to still a hyperactive mind. Its many forms range from total silence to mantras (repeated words or sounds). Learn to practice "mental traffic control" by simply stopping what you are doing at several points during the day or during your practice, and have silence for one or two minutes. Such a discipline can make a huge difference to your performance. Meditation is known to focus the mind, to calm the body, and even to lower blood pressure. Many people practice meditation to alleviate their stress.

SLEEP

Performers who are on the road all the time will testify to their need for sleep. To be tired night after night when expecting to perform at your best is worse than a nightmare. Your body requires sleep to heal itself and to keep you mentally alert. When you lose sleep over a period of time, your body and mind become sluggish and you are unable to think clearly. Sitting in front of a computer all day and night is a recipe for developing poor sleeping patterns. Although different people need varying amounts of sleep, the important thing is that you get sound, restful sleep most nights. Some things that contribute to healthy sleep patterns are moderate exercise during the day, relaxation and quiet time before going to bed, keeping regular hours, and avoiding heavy meals, caffeine, or alcohol just before bedtime.

NUTRITION

Your body is tolerant of what you put in it for a while. Eventually, however, it will complain and threaten to stop working well if you continue to eat poorly. Your body works hard to keep itself balanced chemically, and everything you take in either sustains or alters that balance. Imagine if you kept pouring gasoline with a little bit of water in it each time you refilled your car. Over time it would simply stop. The body tries to let you know by not performing well, hurting, getting lots of colds, and so on. It is when you do not hear or heed the message that the body becomes very insistent on a change of lifestyle by having something dramatic occur.

Your body requires plenty of water. More than 70 percent of your body is water, and what is lost on a daily basis has to be replenished. Pure water is needed, not just any form of fluid. (The body tends to regard other fluids as food and to treat them differently from water.) For performers, the lubrication of the throat and vocal folds is very important.

Make sure you are well hydrated before important events like concerts. Drink water offstage during the intermission or during breaks. Carry it onstage only if you are having some kind of vocal problem or sore throat.

Foods that contain high water content are considered very healthy. This includes most fruits and vegetables. However, a diet of only fruit and vegetables does not give us enough muscle-building protein. Protein comes in many forms, so you are able to choose freely from meat, cheese, yogurt, milk, nuts, seeds, and legumes (beans, lentils, etc.). Grains and some fat are important as well. No matter what your budget, healthy food options are available. Food supplements and vitamins may help when there is little fresh produce. The key is always balance. The same food day after day is not helpful or appetizing.

EXERCISE

There is appropriate exercise for everyone's level of fitness. The simplest thing you can do is walk briskly. It is not unusual for persons who live in large cities to walk at least a mile or two a day. In most cities and towns, however, walking to work or school is not a viable option and a car is essential. This is why gyms and local sports clubs are so popular.

Today many forms of exercise are available that work with the mind as well as the body. Some of the most effective forms of techniques and exercise for vocal performers are these:

- The Alexander technique is a way of balancing mind and body through developing efficient mental and physical habits for daily living. This may include sitting, standing, and walking with minimal effort and a thought process that involves not doing, but being.
- The Feldenkrais method offers a very effective way to correct your body through micromovements that do not take you beyond comfortable limits. Extending your boundaries is a matter of not doing it the "old" way.
- A Pilates routine involves exercises for balancing the body and correcting physical problems, especially alignment and the abdominal muscles. Originally it was developed to help dancers who were injured.
- Tai Chi, a beautiful flowing Eastern martial art form, is ideal for performers because of the almost silky ease of movement it encourages. It is a form of moving meditation, and it provides plenty of mental and physical exercise.

- Chi Gung involves a combination of movement, breathing, and meditation. It is particularly useful for breathing and a quiet state of mind and body.
- Yoga comes in forms such as Raja Yoga (mental) and Hatha Yoga (physical), among many others. It is helpful for posture, breathing, and general well-being.
- Dance in many forms, such as jazz, ballroom, salsa, tap, ballet, circle dancing, and square dancing, increases your rhythm and helps you have fun at the same time.

Your school or community may offer many of these forms of exercise. The internet is full of information about any of them. New websites are springing up constantly. Take the time to explore what is happening in your area.

Active exercises that jar and shake the body or make you pant and gasp can be fun and use up lots of energy. However, they may not be helpful just before you use your voice. Jogging in cold air just before a rehearsal is not a good idea, because breathing cold air through the mouth can make your vocal folds dry and cold. It is not easy to use your voice for a while after a run like that.

Healthy Vocal Habits

Your vocal health will be enhanced or damaged on a daily basis, depending on how you use your voice for speaking and singing. By paying attention to your posture and breathing, you can keep yourself out of vocal trouble.

Chapter 11 included information on how to practice. Go back and remind yourself of that information now. Wisely spent rehearsal time is vital to your vocal health and learning. Short practice sessions are advisable for the beginning singer or actor. Just as you would not go out and run a mile or run for an hour if you had never run before, you would not sing for an hour either.

Being methodical and patient is the best way to learn to use your voice well.

HABITS THAT HARM THE VOICE

All of us, at sometime, have developed habits that harm our voices. Becoming aware of them is the first step toward resolving these habits and replacing them with healthy ones.

POOR VOICE USE

Yelling or shouting is at the top of the list of vocal abuses. Prolonged yelling puts a lot of pressure on the vocal folds and causes them to swell. The resulting hoarseness is called laryngitis. It is analogous to spraining your ankle—except that it afflicts your voice. Since it is not possible to wrap it up and protect it, you need to rest your voice until the swelling has subsided. Unbounded enthusiasm is commendable, but vocalizing it is not recommended for healthy vocal folds.

Talking over loud noise and dance music can also create vocal problems. There is a catch-22 situation here. Music is playing, and people talk over it. Someone then can't hear the music, so the volume is turned up. People talk even louder. The music is turned up again. And so it goes on until everyone is shouting. The next morning scores of people are hoarse, have very tired throats, and have been somewhat deafened.

Constant throat clearing is another source of vocal abuse. People who do this are often unaware of their habit. Clearing the throat makes the vocal folds virtually explode air and can cause damage in the long term. Ask your friends to let you know if you are constantly clearing your throat. It is common for speakers to clear their throats just before they begin to speak, and nervous singers tend to do this before they sing. Most of the time it is not necessary to clear the throat. When you feel the urge to clear, it is best to swallow or drink water instead.

AIRBORNE SUBSTANCES THAT IMPAIR THE VOICE

The job of the vocal folds is to protect your lungs. These folds are so sensitive that inhaling anything larger than three microns (much smaller than a speck of dust) in diameter causes you to cough. As further protection, there are tiny hairs called cilia attached to the cells that line the windpipe and lungs. They beat upward to clear any debris from your lungs. Tiny airborne toxins are able to pass by the vocal folds, inflicting untold damage on the cells that line the respiratory tract, and embed themselves in the cellular structure of your lungs. Over time the cells lose their protective capacity, and disease processes have a clear path. This is particularly true if you smoke anything.

The toxicity of cigarettes is well documented, and new evidence regarding cannabis is frightening. Both smoking and passive or secondhand smoking are considered unhealthy. The message for voice professionals is "Don't smoke!" It is not helpful to your health or vocal career.

You do not always have a choice about where you live and work—it might have to be in smoky nightclubs or toxic big cities. Make it a point to live in the cleanest environment possible. Keep your personal environment free of smoke, fumes, dust, and damp. At least you will avoid compounding the problem by adding your own pollution.

INGESTION OF TOXIC SUBSTANCES

Your body is working constantly to maintain its chemical balance. When you introduce substances that alter that balance, the body works hard to get rid of them. The broad category of recreational drugs is considered destructive to the body in general—especially in large amounts.

Alcohol

Moderation is always a good rule to follow. Your liver is the organ responsible for clearing toxins from your body, and a large amount of alcohol can create damage to your liver. You can read many studies about alcohol. Some of these recommend a glass of wine every night; others tell you it is deadly. However, all tend to agree that getting drunk kills brain cells, slows your responses for nearly twenty-four hours, and plays havoc with your liver. Too much alcohol makes it difficult to speak clearly, sing on pitch, or respond easily to your music.

Alcohol has a drying effect on the mucous membranes that line the throat and larynx. Over time the dryness can become chronic, and the husky "drinker's voice" then emerges. For persons serious about their voice, heavy drinking is not an option. Contrary to some beliefs, it does not help you perform better or truly calm your nerves. It can cause you to perceive that you are performing better, but it is more likely to relax the muscles enough to create pitch and perception problems.

Hard Drugs

There are times when we all want to escape the unpleasant events in our lives. However, drugs like cocaine, opium derivatives, ecstasy, and any other variations will only defer our problems; they don't solve them. A performer, like an athlete, needs all senses and facilities available for the best performance.

COMMON PROBLEMS THAT NEED PROFESSIONAL HELP

Even though we can work to establish healthy vocal habits and avoid harmful ones, vocal problems can occur. When they do, such problems require professional attention.

This section discusses some common issues and typical problems encountered by voice professionals. It does not pretend to be a definitive medical statement or a tool for diagnosis, but merely presents some general information. For more specific knowledge, consult a specialist, refer to the materials listed in "Further Reading," or go onto the internet. When you have any doubts about the way you are feeling or singing, it is best to consult a health professional.

Hoarseness

"Hoarseness" is a catch-all term that can cover a multitude of vocal problems. It occurs when there is any kind of swelling on the vocal folds that causes them to touch with uneven surfaces. It becomes a problem only when it does not go away. Then you have to begin to search for possible causes. The following can cause temporary hoarseness:

- poor speech habits
- oversinging or singing or speaking too loudly
- singing with a forced straight tone for long hours (some choirs)
- singing for too many hours in one day
- air-conditioning
- air travel
- central heating with low humidity
- constant throat clearing
- drinking too much alcohol
- medications such as decongestants that dry the throat
- medications like aspirin and ibuprofen that cause local bleeding
- smoking
- fatigue
- your menstrual period

- sore throat
- cold or flu

Paying attention to vocal technique, resting, drinking plenty of water, getting a good night's sleep, and humidifying your environment can help most of the problems above. If you experience hoarseness after practicing or a choral rehearsal, it will normally go away after a few hours. It is not unusual to oversing in a choral situation. If hoarseness occurs after every rehearsal, however, you would do well to go to your teacher and look at what you might be doing vocally to cause this.

Air Travel

The incredible dryness experienced during flying can cause all kinds of respiratory symptoms. You are advised to drink lots of water. It is wise to breathe through a wet cloth or mask during the flight as well. Many professional performers even take surgeon's masks and wet them. Not only does this prevent your throat and lungs from becoming too dry; it also acts as an extra air filter. People around you may think you a little weird, but (as long as your mask is not black) it is well worth the strange looks. This can make all the difference in how you feel when you land.

Excess Fluid during Menstrual Cycles

During the menstrual period it is common for excess fluid to be present in many of the tissues of the body, including the vocal folds. This swelling makes you feel heavy and dull. You may even sound hoarse from the swelling on the vocal folds. It is best to sing gently on those days and take easy physical exercise when you can. Often vocalizing makes you feel better.

EXTENDED OR LINGERING HOARSENESS

As a general rule, when you are hoarse for more than two weeks, seek professional advice. There can be any number of benign causes for this, so it is best not to be your own diagnostician. The problem can be systemic or localized in the vocal or respiratory tracts.

ALLERGIES

There are so many types of allergies—owing to dust, pollen and smoke, food intolerances, and reactions to medicines—that determining the cause is not always easy. It is not fun to live with streaming eyes and stuffy noses, or with gallons of phlegm. If the allergy is seasonal, you can get some relief in the off-season. However, when your symptoms continue unabated, it is time to see a doctor or other health practitioner. The allergens usually create a buildup of histamines. Therefore many people are given antihistamine medication for allergies. Some of these medications are also combined with decongestants and have an extremely drying effect on the mucous membranes of the nose and throat. Always let your doctor know that you are a performer, so that he can give you the most appropriate medication.

LARYNGITIS

Laryngitis is inflammation of the vocal folds and surrounding tissue. It can be bacterial or viral. You can tell the difference by the color of what you are coughing up. If it is greenish and foul-looking, it is usually bacterial, and some medication might be in order. Viral laryngitis is *not usually helped* by any medication. You can help yourself by keeping the throat moist at all times and remaining quiet. Drinking lots of water and keeping your room humidified is important for your comfort. (Make sure you clean your humidifier periodically. That dampness can harbor all kinds of bugs and bacteria.) Inhaling of steam is suggested by many doctors and highly effective in the healing process.

SINUSITIS

Although the sinuses do not help our voice very much, they can produce a lot of discomfort when they are infected. Sinus problems can cause headaches, make you feel heavy-headed, and create a postnasal drip that makes you hoarse. Again, bringing up foul-colored mucus implies infection and indicates the need for professional help. Decongestants can allay the symptoms by helping you breathe more easily, but may cause excessive drying of the throat and a dependence on the medication. It is unwise to take decongestants over a long period of time.

PERSISTENT SORE THROAT

Like hoarseness, sore throats can stem from a variety of problems. They can be symptomatic of viral or bacterial infection, tonsillitis, sinusitis, and postnasal drip. When you have a sore throat, it is wise to maintain short rehearsals and take good care of your voice. If you overwork your voice while you have a sore throat, you run the risk of developing hoarseness.

COUGHING DURING AND AFTER A RESPIRATORY PROBLEM

Coughing can be very violent and hard on the vocal folds. It is a normal reflex associated with the respiratory system, which does not like to have foreign substances in it, and coughing is one way of getting rid of them. The problem is created when the cough lingers after the apparent disease is gone. Your vocal folds will still have swelling because of the coughing, and using your voice can provoke even more coughing. It is a catch-22 situation, and you need to be careful during this time period.

Test your voice with gentle hums and *ng*'s within a short vocal range after the coughing has stopped. However, you may find that it will take as long as two weeks for the vocal folds to become normal after prolonged coughing. This is a good time to employ your visualization and silent practice.

VOCAL NODULES

When people sing or speak with excessive tension or poor vocal technique, they abuse the vocal folds. The vocal folds bang together and create a swelling like a callus or a corn on the inner edges (see figure 12.1). This may begin as a blood clot and slowly develop into something firmer and larger. The swelling or nodule prevents the vocal folds from touching cleanly and allows excess air through the resulting chink. The symptom is constant hoarseness or breathiness throughout the speaking and singing voice. There is loss of vocal range and a tendency for the voice to sound breathy, weak, and tired.

When nodules are discovered early enough, they can be corrected by voice and/or speech therapy. An ear, nose, and throat specialist will probably suggest that they be surgically removed if they are large and hard. Good vocal technique is the way to prevent and correct vocal nodules. Removing the nodules surgically will only remove the symptoms and may leave scar tissue. Vocal nodules will return if you continue the same vocal habits. Many

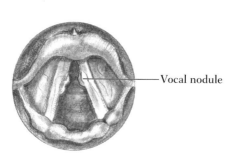

Vocal nodule

FIGURE 12.1
Vocal nodules

budding vocal careers have been ruined by poor technique—no matter what the singing style.

Hoarseness will usually be the first symptom of vocal abuse. There are very few pain fibers in the larynx, and it has no obvious way of letting you know you are in trouble. If you are having constant throat pain and vocal fatigue, you need to do something immediately.

VOCAL FATIGUE

Your voice can be overworked over a long time to the point of muscle fatigue. Tired vocal muscles, like any other muscle of the body, simply refuse to do what you want. One symptom of vocal fatigue is a wobble in the sound. By the time vocal fatigue sets in, the vocal folds are usually very damaged. This is a serious symptom, not easily corrected. If you are at the beginning of your vocal studies, this is not a likely problem. It could become one if you have been singing incorrectly for some time or regularly abusing your voice or your body. It is worth noting that your voice will not stand constant abuse without eventually rebelling. The moment it chooses to rebel may not be the most opportune one for you. Classroom teachers yelling over noisy students and those shouting over constant noise are prone to this problem. Changing your work environment may be necessary if you want your voice to last your lifetime.

ACID REFLUX

Acid reflux is more common in older people, but it can happen to anyone at any age. Reflux typically happens during sleep when stomach acids are regurgitated. The acid secreted is a very potent hydrochloric acid that irritates and burns everything it touches. If you have ever wondered what the burning sensation was after you vomited, it was this acid. Reflux is not pleasant and is very harmful to the larynx. The symptoms include waking up with a burning throat that goes away during the day, foul breath (more than your normal bad breath), and hoarseness. People with this problem are usually given special diets, instructed not to eat a heavy meal late at night, advised to keep the head more elevated at night, and prescribed medication to neutralize the acid. If you think you have reflux, see your doctor.

HEARING AND NOISE POLLUTION

Many people live in noisy environments—busy streets, traffic, loud TVs and stereos, personal stereos and headphones, slamming doors, and loud concerts. We have almost become immune to the amount of loud noise that constantly surrounds us. It is making us deaf slowly.

The eardrum functions to protect the ear and transmit sound signals to your brain. However, its protective capacity is damaged every time you overload it with loud sustained noise. After a rock concert, it takes the ear several days to recover from the trauma. You may notice that you hear poorly the day after attending such concerts. Wearing earplugs to them is worth your consideration.

Loud noise causes people to develop partial hearing impairment because of exposure to excessive decibel levels—for example, in dance clubs, at rock concerts, at sporting events, or even through car or personal stereos, TVs, and so on. Some clubs are known to have sound at the decibel levels of a jet plane. Sound is considered harmful when it reaches 90 decibels. A jet plane takes off at 120 decibels. That is approximately 30 decibels over the hearing health limit. (Decibels go up by the power of ten, so you can work out just how loud 120 decibels might be.) The ears are an important part of singing and integral to the ability to hear. They are traumatized by long sessions of loud music. If your hearing is impaired, your voice could be too, because sensitivity to language, vocal feedback, and pitch perception will be reduced.

OPTIONAL TREATMENTS

A number of options are available for treating some of the health problems discussed above. In addition to standard medical treatment, many people find help in homeopathy, naturopathy, acupuncture, and nutrition and other therapies. If you find you are taking medication on a long-term basis, seek further answers from a health care professional regarding your problem.

MAINTAINING YOUR VOICE FOR LIFE

Your voice is precious and an important aspect of your communication. Trying to communicate without sound is an extremely frustrating and slow process. There are few, if any, jobs where no talking is involved. Singing or speaking while under vocal duress is counterproductive and vocally risky. This chapter has offered a variety of suggestions for preventing vocal ill health and maintaining a healthy voice.

A positive spirit and a healthy lifestyle are the two most important things you can maintain for yourself and your voice. Paying attention to your attitudes, general health and fitness, and practice habits will provide you with vocal health and the confidence to use your voice and your body wisely in performance and for the rest of your life.

Summary of Part III

Stage presence and your love of performing combined with a reliable vocal technique will give you and your audiences hours of pleasure. Your journey to gain the ability to be effective at your profession may seem long to you. To your audience, it all seems very natural and easy. Oh, that it were so! Only you can know the journey you have taken to performance. Appreciate all the ups and downs along the way, and be thankful for where you are.

The ideas and thoughts offered in part III were intended to give you food for further thought and create ways for you to enjoy the process of new discoveries about your ability to perform. You may have heard many of these things before, but approaching your performance with vision and a mind open to new experiences will allow you to explore new paths and boundaries—perhaps no boundaries—in terms of sound.

Epilogue

The Complete Performer

If one could venture an anatomical and molecular definition of a complete performer, it might be as follows: a mass of vibrating atoms all with adequate space for movement, each contributing to physical balance and alignment, coordinated respiratory rhythm and vocal fold vibration, a tuned and responsive resonance structure and spontaneous articulation, coupled with the imagination and spirit of the individual.

Were the above to be a requirement for being a performer, there would probably be very few. There are many performers who break the physical rules, yet use their voices well enough to be considered good. Sometimes they succeed because of their spirit and determination and their having been endowed with a beauty of tone in spite of what they are doing physically. They are the lucky ones. Although the physical structure of the vocal instrument is determined at birth, very few performers ever reach the optimal possibilities of its use. On the other hand, it is possible for everyone to sound better with proper attention and guidance.

Many factors determine whether a performer will be good. Even some with seemingly perfect physical features have difficulty singing. Without spirit and imagination, a performer and the message become boring and lifeless. When these two ingredients are engaged, the body is alive and the eyes are focused and indicate "being here," the face is responsive to the meaning of the words, and the performer is fully in the present moment, performing with spontaneity of tone and color.

To use one's voice well, one must know how the voice functions. Armed with such knowledge, the performer, teacher, or therapist can make many adjustments more easily. However, it is just as important to understand that the mind and imagination trigger physical reactions. The complete voice professional or performer needs to have knowledge of the physical aspects, experience of vocal performance, imagination and spontaneity, and the flexibility and ability to listen without preconceptions as tools of his or her trade. The complete performer will pay attention to all of these things and enjoy true freedom of expression. When this happens, the resulting voice will be unforgettable—with a seamless, timeless quality like that of a finely tuned bell whose sound seems to come from everywhere at once, fill the space around it, and heal those who have the privilege of hearing it.

Appendix A

Summary of Anatomical Terminology

Should you wish to look at a medical text, you will have to know anatomical terminology. Inventing new words is not useful when the international scientific community needs to be able to talk to each other. So that anatomists and scientists around the world could easily communicate, they agreed on a common language and system of describing how and where structures are located on the body. They started with anatomical position (see chapter 1). From there they created four imaginary planes passing through the body: three vertical planes, the medial, sagittal, and coronal, and one horizontal or transverse.

THE PLANES OF THE BODY

The planes of the body help anatomists define the location of any structure precisely. It is important to know whether a structure is toward the center or away from it, above or below it, or in front or behind it. Their definitions are as follows:

- The *median plane* passes vertically through the midline of the body, dividing it into equal right and left halves. Any approaching the midline is defined as medial. For example, your nose is medial to your ear. Anything away from the midline is termed lateral. Every structure can have a midline.

- The *sagittal plane* divides the body or the structure into right and left sections, which can be equal or unequal. It is common to see illustrations of the throat in sagittal section. There are several of these in this book.
- The *coronal plane* is a vertical plane that divides the body into front and back (anterior and posterior) portions. These portions do not have to be equal. There is a coronal section of the tongue in chapter 6.
- The *horizontal (transverse) plane* is any plane that passes through the body transversely, dividing the body into upper and lower (superior and inferior) portions.

TERMS OF RELATIONSHIP

All structures of the body are defined in terms of their relationship, whether superficial or deep, anterior or posterior, or medial or lateral.

- *Anterior (ventral, front)* means nearer to the front of the body. The pectoral muscles are located anteriorly. Note: the anterior surface of the hand is called the *palmer* surface, and the upper area of the foot is called the *dorsum* or *dorsal* surface.
- *Posterior (dorsal, behind)* means nearer to or on the back of the body; e.g., the spine is located posteriorly. Note: the posterior surface of the hand is called the *dorsal* surface, and the posterior surface, or sole, of the foot is called the *plantar* surface.
- *Superior (cephalic, cranial, above)* is toward the head or upper part of the body. The shoulders are superior to the hips.
- *Inferior (caudal, below)* means toward the feet or lower part of the body. The hips are inferior to the shoulders.
- *Medial* means toward the median plane or the midline of the body. The nose is medial to the ear, the little finger is medial to the thumb.
- *Lateral* means away from the median plane of the body. The arm is lateral to the trunk and the thumb is lateral to the little finger.

TERMS OF COMPARISON

These terms are used to compare the relative position of two structures to each other.

- *Proximal* refers to the part of the structure nearest to the trunk of the body, or point of origin. For example, the proximal end of the upper arm bone, the humerus, is the end forming a joint with the shoulder.
- *Distal* refers to the part of the structure that is the most distant from the trunk or point of origin. The distal part of the humerus would be the point nearest the elbow.
- *Superficial* means nearer the surface of the skin.
- *Deep* means away, or farther from the surface of the skin.

TERMS CONNECTED WITH MUSCLES

Muscles can cause movement only by contracting. They contract by means of a signal from the nervous system. When that signal is stopped, the muscle releases or relaxes.

- The *prime mover* is the muscle or group of muscles that is contracting to cause the movement.
- The *antagonist* is the opposite of prime mover. This muscle must relax when the prime mover is contracting for complete action.
- A *synergist* is a muscle or groups of muscles working together to stabilize a joint. This means that the muscles on either side of the joint work together to stabilize it. For example, to enable you to stand on one leg, the muscles on the inside and outside of the thigh must work together to keep you from falling.

TERMS THAT DESCRIBE MOVEMENTS OF JOINTS

The muscles that flex a joint are located on the front of the body until you get to the knee. The muscles that extend a joint are located on the back of the body until you get to the knee. Touching your toes involves flexion of the spine forward. Doing a back bend involves extension of the spine backward. Both of these actions require active muscle contraction.

- *Flexion* is, in general, bending or making a decreasing angle between bones, or parts of the body. It causes mainly movement along the front of the body.

- *Extension* is usually the straightening of a joint that is bent; the opposite movement to flexion. A muscle must contract to cause this action. Some people confuse this term with lengthening.

Extension can cause a joint to have an angle as well, as in a back bend or the backward movement of the wrist. Extension causes mainly movement along the back of the body.

- *Abduction* means to move a structure away from the midline.
- *Adduction* means to move a structure toward the midline.
- *Lateral rotation* is to turn a part of the body or a bone away from the midline. For example, turnout of the legs in the hip sockets is important for ballet.
- *Medial rotation* means rotation toward the midline of a part of the body.
- *Circumduction* involves a combination of successive movements of flexion, abduction, extension, and adduction in such a way that the distal end of the part being moved describes a circle (seen in arm and leg movements).
- *Supination* is turning the palm of the hand to face forward.
- *Pronation* is turning the back of the hand to face forward.
- *Eversion* is turning the sole of the foot so that it faces away from the other foot.
- *Inversion* is turning sole of the foot so that it faces toward the other foot.

REVIEW OF NAMING MUSCLES

Muscles are named the following ways:

- Their location in the body: e.g., the pectoral muscles are located in the pectoral or chest area.
- Their shape: e.g., the trapezius on the back.
- Their origin and insertion: e.g., the stylo-glossus (styloid process to tongue).
- Their action: e.g., the levator palati (elevator of the palate).

When several muscles are in a group, they are named according to their relationship with each other. The superior, middle, and inferior pharyngeal constrictors are good examples.

Appendix B

Working with Rhythm

Not only is rhythm inherent in language and in dialect; it is also in your body. Your body is a walking rhythm band with pulse, breath, and even organs having their own beat. The object of these exercises is to help you feel the rhythm inside you rather than a token tapping of a toe or finger.

1. First walk, or march, and clap the basic beat of the song loudly (in 4/4 time this would be four claps; in 3/4 time it would be three claps). Do not bother with the exact rhythm of each phrase yet; just get the feel of the music. Pretend you are clapping with a dance band or pop singers at a concert.
2. Next, begin to singsong or chant the actual rhythm of the song on one pitch, using any syllable such as *lah* or *doo* to this basic beat. Then singsong the words of the song, on one pitch, to the rhythm while walking and clapping. Do not allow your left brain to trap you into lacking courage or stop where you perceive a mistake; just keep walking and clapping. Be aware that when you feel insecure, your body

will want to hesitate. By walking and clapping, you will be able to overcome this tendency. This is why it is not helpful to tap a toe or finger (they are too small and can be bullied easily by your analytical brain). The moment you become unsure, the tapping will stop. Please do not stop until the end of the song! Don't worry about being perfect.

3. A way of checking that you know the exact rhythm is to singsong it in a staccato manner, using any syllable such as *ha* or *la* or *tee* or *hee*. This means that each note is short and sharp and totally disconnected from the note before. Rhythmic mistakes show up quickly when you do this because you are filling in with silence rather than sound.

4. Here is one you can do after you have learned the melody. Sing the song to your own pulse. Find the pulse in your wrist or on your neck. While keeping your finger lightly on your pulse sing a familiar song. Make sure you stay in touch with your own inner beat while singing. If you find you cannot feel your pulse, you have probably allowed physical tension to interfere.

Further Reading

Adams, David. *A Handbook of Diction for Singers: Italian, German, French*. New York: Oxford University Press, 1999.

Alexander, F. Matthias. *The Alexander Technique: The Writings of F. Matthias Alexander*. Selected by Edward Maisil. London: Thames & Hudson, 1990.

Berendt, Joachim Ernst. *Nada Brahma: The World Is Sound*. London: East-West Publications, 1988.

Bunch, Meribeth. *Dynamics of the Singing Voice*. 4th ed. New York: Sprinter-Verlag, 1997.

Bunch, Meribeth, and Cynthia Vaughn. *The Singing Book*. New York: W. W. Norton, 2004.

Calais-Germain, Blandine. *Anatomy of Movement*. Seattle: Eastland Press, 1993.

Caldwell, Robert. *The Performer Prepares*. Redland, Wash.: Caldwell Publishing, 1990.

Conable, Barbara. *The Structures and Movement of Breathing*. Chicago: GIA Publications, 2000.

Conable, Barbara, and Benjamin Conable. *What Every Musician Needs to Know about the Body: The Practical Application of Body Mapping and the Alexander Technique to Making Music.* Portland, Oreg.: Andover Press, 2000.

Craig, David. *A Performer Prepares: A Guide to Song Preparation for Actors, Singers and Dancers.* New York: Applause Theatre Book Publishers, 1999.

Dennison, Paul E. *Brain-Gym.* Ventura, Calif.: Edu-Kinesthetics, 1986.

Diamond, John. *The Life Energy in Music.* 3 Vols. New York: Archaeus Press, 1983.

Emmons, Shirlee, and Alma Thomas. *Power Performance for Singers: Transcending the Barriers.* New York: Oxford University Press, 1998.

Goldsmith, Joan Oliver. *How Can We Keep from Singing?: Music and the Passionate Life.* New York: W. W. Norton, 2001.

Govinda, Anagarika. *Creative Meditation and Multidimensional Consciousness.* London: Unwin Paperbacks, 1977.

Kimball, Carol. *SONG: A Guide to Style and Literature.* Redland, Wash.: Caldwell Publishing, 1996.

Macdonald, Glynn. *Illustrated Elements of Alexander Technique.* London: Element, 2002.

Nelson, Samuel H., and Elizabeth Blades-Zeller. *Singing with Your Whole Self: The Feldenkrais Method and Voice.* Rochester, N.Y.: Inspiration Press, 2000.

Netter, Frank H. *Atlas of Human Anatomy.* Summit, N.J.: Novartis Education Publishers, 2003.

Promislow, Sharon. *Making the Brain/Body Connection.* West Vancouver, Can.: Kinetic Publishing, 1999.

Ristad, Eloise. *A Soprano on Her Head: Right-Side-Up Reflections on Life and Other Performances.* Moab, Utah: Real People Press, 1982.

Sataloff, Robert Thayer. *Vocal Health and Pedagogy.* San Diego: Singular Publishing, 1998.

Titze, Ingo R. *Principles of Voice Production.* Englewood Cliffs, N.J.: Prentice-Hall, 1994.

Tolle, Eckhart. *The Power of Now: A Guide to Spiritual Enlightenment.* Novato, Calif.: New World Library, 1999; pb ed., 2004.

Tomatis, Alfred A. *The Conscious Ear: My Life of Transformation through Listening.* Barrytown, N.Y.: Station Hill Press, 1991.

Vennard, William. *Singing, the Mechanism and the Technic.* Rev. ed. New York: Carl Fischer, 1967.

Zander, Rosamund S., and Benjamin Zander. *The Art of Possibility: Transforming Professional and Personal Life.* Boston: Harvard Business School Press, 2000.

Index